INVASION OF PRIVACY

Berkley Books by Louis R. Mizell, Jr.

INVASION OF PRIVACY

STREET SENSE FOR PARENTS

STREET SENSE FOR SENIORS

STREET SENSE FOR STUDENTS

STREET SENSE FOR WOMEN

INVASION
OF
PRIVACY

LOUIS R. MIZELL, JR.

BERKLEY BOOKS, NEW YORK

This book is an original publication of The Berkley Publishing Group.

INVASION OF PRIVACY

A Berkley Book / published by arrangement with
the author

PRINTING HISTORY
Berkley trade paperback edition / June 1998

The Penguin Putnam Inc. World Wide Web site address is
http://www.penguinputnam.com

ISBN: 0-425-16088-2

BERKLEY®
Berkley Books are published by The Berkley Publishing Group,
a member of Penguin Putnam Inc.,
200 Madison Avenue, New York, New York 10016.
BERKLEY and the "B" design
are trademarks belonging to Berkley Publishing Corporation.

PRINTED IN THE UNITED STATES OF AMERICA

10 9 8 7 6 5 4 3 2 1

For

Becky Boyd and Patrick Friel

ACKNOWLEDGMENTS

Concerned that our right to privacy, one of our most precious freedoms, is being seriously threatened, more than two hundred people volunteered their time, expertise, and personal experiences to make this book possible. To these people I would like to say thank you. I salute your professionalism and dedication and very much appreciate your contributions.

Convinced that *Invasion of Privacy* was a much-needed and important book, Natalee Rosenstein, Donna Gould, and the hard-charging Berkley Publishing team yelled, "Write it," and provided their enthusiastic support. Becky Boyd, my office manager, confidante, and friend, masterfully juggled a dozen duties at once, kept the office organized, and is credited with keeping us all sane. Tenacious and fun to work with, John Willig, my energetic literary agent, nurtured every page of this project. Bringing thirty years of security experience to the book, my partner Peter Roche provided much appreciated encouragement and many useful suggestions and sources. Talented beyond her years, Honor Spire, a graduate of the University of Vermont, greatly impressed me with her work ethic and her advanced research and writing skills. Providing up-to-date advice, Ernesto Brown, a computer systems analyst, taught us how hackers are stealing private information and how we can prevent this theft. Kevin Lamb, researcher/investigator extraordinaire, uncovered information others could not find. Bringing her Ph.D. in psychology and knowledge of four languages to the office, Bea Dixon added much-appreciated class

Acknowledgments

and insight to this book. Wrestling with mountains of newspapers and source reports, Noreen Beavers developed a privacy database second to none. Spunky and disciplined, Ericka Walters, the youngest member of my staff, stands as a role model for all teenagers. Maggie Watt, a tribute to the nursing profession, analyzed our medical information and provided valuable comments. Tirelessly perusing scores of newspapers each day, Beverly Reed made sure that this book was relevant to readers in all fifty states. And a special thanks to my friend and partner, Lisa Fentress, a top-notch lawyer, professional, and athlete.

As with most books, many unsung heros contributed invaluable time, spirit, and professionalism to *Invasion of Privacy.* I genuinely believe that the efforts of these individuals will help all of us retain our right to privacy. Thank you, thank you, thank you: Alice M. Clark, Christina Nunez, Elizabeth Brenden, John Healy, Patricia Ginalick, Carol Ann Rodier, Alice Miller, Stacey Perkal, James Washington, Bob Stuber, Jack Gottschalk, Kathleen Trepper, Liz Boyle, Victoria Brown, Jack Plaxe, Patty Raine, Catherine Craun, Brenda Brewer, Donna Lewis, Hilary Wright, Don Moss, Jim Grady, Carol Stricker, Suzanne Conway, Maureen Becker, and Jamie Smith.

Special thanks and respect to my many friends at the CIA, the U.S. Department of State, and the FBI.

CONTENTS

Contents

CONTENTS

INTRODUCTION

While conversing with a group of men and women in the lobby of an upscale health club, my attention turned suddenly to a new member, a strikingly beautiful woman, who had just walked by. "She's pretty, Lou, but you sure don't want to date her," whispered a woman who had been standing at my left shoulder. "She's got a screaming case of herpes."

Stunned by the cattiness and the inappropriateness of the woman's comment, I asked, "How do you know?"

"Because I work at the clinic where she's getting treatment," the woman nonchalantly explained.

It was that insensitive comment and a comment I would hear one month later that gave me the impetus to write a book on privacy.

The second inspiration occurred at a retirement party for a Marine Corps colonel, a buddy with whom I served in Vietnam. "You'd better get your antisocial ass to my retirement party," my friend growled, knowing full well that I was not wild about parties. We had been through so much together that he also knew I wouldn't say no.

As I snuggled up to the hors d'oeuvres, blocking the rest of the herd from the feeding trough, a balding man in his late thirties engaged me in conversation. "I hear you have kind of an unusual job, writing books and chasing fugitives and stuff," he said as I put another pound of meatballs on my plate.

"Yeah, I really like it," I responded half choking between swallows. "Every morning I bound out of bed and think, *Where else could a grown man have so much fun?* What do you do?" I asked, trying to divert attention from myself.

"I'm an agent for the Internal Revenue Service," he answered proudly, wiping white crab dip from the sleeve of his tweed coat. "Just let me know if you need any information on anybody," he offered, handing me his business card. "I'll look it up on the computer . . . just don't tell anyone where you got it."

My first response was, "Hey great, thanks, I'd really appreciate that!" and then I went back to hogging the hors d'oeuvres. But then I started thinking: *Now wait a minute, can this guy just push a button and view* my *tax records? What right does he have offering me the inside scoop on someone else's confidential tax forms? Hey, I don't like this!* And thus began a book on privacy.

On July 18, 1994, Senator John Glenn, chairman of the Senate Governmental Affairs Committee, announced that more than 1,300 employees of the Internal Revenue Service had been investigated for using government computers to browse through the confidential tax records of friends, relatives, neighbors, celebrities, and complete strangers. It is not known how many of the 115,000 IRS employees have illegally perused tax records without being caught.

Dishonest and unethical insiders pose one of the greatest threats to privacy.

In 1996, ten employees of the Social Security Administration were caught passing confidential information on more than eleven thousand citizens to a credit card fraud ring. Considered to be one of the biggest breaches of security of personal data held by the federal government, the employees plugged Social Security numbers (the key to one's financial soul) into a government computer and provided the crooks with birth dates, addresses, and mothers' maiden names—private information legitimate customers would use to activate new credit cards.

Bank officials estimated that the goods, services, and cash withdrawals billed to the stolen cards totaled $10 million.

The thieves bribed the Social Security employees, whom they knew socially, with payoffs of $10 to $75. The invasion of privacy cost society—we who are the taxpayers—$10 million and landed over eleven thousand honest, hardworking citizens in credit hell.

Snooping and selling our private information, dangerous insiders can be found at almost every government and private organization including the U.S. Postal Service, credit companies, law enforcement agencies, telephone companies, banks, and the Department of Motor Vehicles. In 1996, a nurse at the Maryland Shock Trauma Center was sentenced to ten years in prison for using a hospital computer to steal credit information from a critically wounded police officer. The nurse used the data to obtain five credit cards in the officer's name and then charged $52,485 in purchases and cash advances. The officer was hospitalized with three gunshot wounds. Four months later, an employee of an East Coast medical examiner's office was charged with cleaning out the checking account of a dead man whose body he delivered to the morgue.

In Houston, Texas, police arrested an employee of a telephone company and charged her with selling confidential customer information, including unpublished names, phone numbers, addresses, and Social Security numbers, to a bank fraud suspect. The inside information enabled the criminal to defraud banks and telephone company customers of tens of thousands of dollars.

Should data bankers and other marketers be allowed to compile a list of frequent callers to divorce lawyers and sell that list to dating services, psychologists, real estate agents, and financial advisors? Should an antiabortion group be allowed to collect the phone numbers of women who call abortion clinics? Should a pharmaceutical company be able to obtain the names and numbers of people who call proctologists and dermatologists?

Telephone records—the telephone numbers customers call and the phone numbers of the people who call the customer—are increasingly being obtained and analyzed by telephone companies, computer hackers, data brokers, stalkers, and other criminals.

Many customers of the telephone company MCI were furious to learn that the company had peeked at their personal phone records to get the names of people they called who did not subscribe to MCI services. MCI then sent promotional materials to the non-MCI subscribers implying that the MCI customer felt it was in their interest to switch long-distance services.

There are many known cases in which telephone companies and renegade insiders have provided outside interests with customer phone records and other private information. There are also many cases in which phone company employees illegally listened to their customers' telephone conversations.

Invasion of privacy horror stories—legal and illegal—abound at the Department of Motor Vehicles (DMV). Actress Rebecca Schaeffer was murdered by a crazed fan who had no problem obtaining her unlisted address from the DMV.

A female psychiatric social worker was forced to drop a patient after he threatened to rape her. The patient would later obtain her unlisted address from the DMV and set her house on fire. The social worker's husband was killed in the blaze and she suffered horrible burns over 80 percent of her body.

There are even cases in which the DMV has provided confidential information to incarcerated stalkers and other criminals. In California, a woman was obsessively stalked by a man who threatened to kill her and to rape her young daughter. When the man was finally sent to prison for murder of an apartment manager and rape of an eleven-year-old girl, the woman moved to an undisclosed location. But the incarcerated stalker wrote a letter to the DMV claiming that the woman was a witness to an accident. Incredibly, the DMV sent the woman's new address to the prisoner. The DMV clerk even put the prisoner's ID number on the envelope.

Leaked personal information can be used in a dozen different ways by a dozen different criminals.

An employee of the DMV in Washington, D.C., used the private data of thirty-three motorists—names, addresses, birth dates, and Social Security numbers—to create bogus licenses. The licenses were used to obtain credit cards and to establish credit at jewelry and department stores. Tens of thousands of dollars were charged to the unwitting and innocent motorists.

One man who had been shot used the phony license at a hospital. The hospital mailed a bill to the address listed on the wounded man's driver's license. The man who received the bill naturally refused to pay it because he had never been in the hospital. The incident damaged the innocent man's credit.

Another victim, an associate producer for the television show *America's Most Wanted*, received a summons to appear in court for six serious driving violations. The busy producer had to make dozens of phone calls, write letters, and spend many hours of his own time trying to get the situation straightened out. The real offender was never caught and may still be using the producer's good name to commit crimes.

Motor vehicle records are available from a wide range of sources. In Massachusetts, a number of rental car agencies are creating a computer linkup with the Registry of Motor Vehicles. Every clerk and administrator at these agencies will have access to a customer's driving history and other pertinent data. "In the first place," said one privacy advocate, "how do we know they will only snoop at *customer's* records?"

"I know this really strange guy who works at the rental agency," said a twenty-six-year-old woman. "I'd hate for him to know my address, phone number, and license tag."

The issue of privacy is not one topic or even ten topics. It is a hundred topics.

Since I still do classified work for the government and some multinational corporations, I am occasionally polygraphed and have to have my background investigation periodically updated. As a former federal officer, I recognize that this is important. But I would be furious if this sensitive file were leaked to unauthorized individuals, used for political purposes, or if it contained inaccurate information.

Following one update, the government investigator called me in and said that they were uncomfortable with what appeared to be "an obsession with pornographic adult movies."

"What in the world are you talking about?" I responded, genuinely bewildered. I had seen my share of X-rated movies while in college twenty years earlier (and have been in a lot of ports and a lot of back-alley bars) but I certainly was not obsessed with any of my vices.

As it turned out, three of my roommates in a group

house had been using my movie rental card during a time when I was traveling to eighty-seven countries for the government. The investigator had obtained my video rental record but failed to notice that the signatures were not in my handwriting and that I was in Lebanon, El Salvador, and Nepal at the time the movies were rented.

What if I had not been confronted? Would the investigator's inaccurate analysis be in my record? Would an employer see the inaccurate information and treat me like a pariah? Would the word be whispered about that I was a bit kinky? And what right does a video store have to divulge my rental habits? Who else have they given that information to?

When a twenty-two-year-old Duke University student, a cardholder with a national video rental chain, traveled to Virginia to visit her mother, she used her card to rent a movie. The rental clerk, "a really creepy guy," entered the card into the computer and presto, he suddenly knew her address and phone number in North Carolina, her Social Security number, and the location of her part-time job. "It bothered me that a complete stranger hundreds of miles from home would have access to that information," she said. It bothered her a lot more when the "creepy" guy called her a week later in North Carolina.

During 1996, the grapevine in Washington, D.C., was abuzz with gossip about a certain celebrity couple who were undergoing a hotly contested divorce. The wife, who had moved to New York, was communicating with her lawyer in D.C. with a facsimile machine.

Unbeknownst to the wife, the lawyer had a communal office arrangement that involved sharing the facsimile and other equipment with other offices.

To my knowledge, the wife, the husband, and the lawyer never learned that a dozen other people were reading her highly confidential faxes, which sometimes sat for hours before being retrieved. The faxes reportedly described the most lurid details of their relationship including the husband's very unusual sexual preferences.

It is no secret that computers, as wonderful as they are, are responsible for some of the worst privacy nightmares. In hundreds of thousands of cases, hackers have stolen sensitive information from computers and provided the data to who knows who. In thousands of cases, people with legitimate access to databases have abused their privilege and leaked private information. And in thousands of known cases, thieves have taken the low-tech route and simply walked out the door with the entire computer.

On November 8, 1996, a computer containing information on 314,000 credit card accounts, including Visa, MasterCard, and American Express, was stolen from a Visa International office in New York.

In Florida, an investigator assigned to the Florida Department of Health and Rehabilitative Services (HRS) was fired for stealing a confidential computer disk containing the names of 4,000 AIDS patients and sharing the private information with unauthorized outsiders.

As Big Brother continues to get bigger and the surveillance cameras continue to get smaller, secret videotaping has evolved into the single greatest threat to personal privacy.

The chapter "Secret Videotaping" reviews scores of cases in which people have been secretly filmed while using a public bathroom, showering at health clubs, changing clothes in locker rooms and dressing rooms, and while making love.

Most people will be surprised to learn that the perpetrators of surreptitious surveillance include politicians, movie stars, lawyers, doctors, teachers, police officers, and members of the clergy.

A repugnant, highly offensive invasion of privacy, secret videotaping is increasingly occurring in private homes (unbeknownst to the residents), high schools and colleges, hotels, department store dressing rooms, hospitals, and offices. Thousands of these degrading tapes of innocent and unsuspecting citizens have been distributed and even advertised for sale on the Internet.

Betraying the most intimate trust, there are hundreds of known cases in which men (usually) have secretly videotaped their own or someone else's lovemaking. In most of these cases the woman, the unwitting victim, is the last to learn that a degrading tape of her lovemaking has been distributed, repeatedly copied, and viewed by scores of strangers.

Even the most sophisticated readers will be shocked to learn how easy it is to intercept cellular phone calls and to steal voice mail and E-mail messages—and how frequently these interceptions occur.

More than 100,000 men and women receive obscene or harassing phone calls every day in the United States. Entering homes and offices uninvited, the obscene phone caller is a faceless monster who murders serenity, commits emotional rape, and destroys our sense of privacy. The chapter "Obscene and Harassing Phone Calls" discusses several infamous cases and teaches potential victims how to handle such calls.

As the chapter "Listening Devices" illustrates, technological advances in recent years have spawned spying devices that put James Bond's glittering gadgetry and Maxwell Smart's shoe-phone to shame. Companies are bugging competitors, employers are bugging employees, and lovers are bugging one another. Listening devices are being concealed in briefcases, telephones, calculators, and pens.

A pedophile who was having a sexual relationship with a fourteen-year-old girl gave her a clock radio as a present. The radio contained a listening device so he would know if the girl discussed their relationship with her parents.

The scariest and most eye-opening chapter in this book may very well be "Privacy and the Medical Industry."

In Florida, a hospital gave computer software to an outside fund-raising group that allowed them unlimited access to 12,000 patient files. The patients were furious to learn that the fund-raisers were reviewing every detail of their confidential medical, financial, and personal records without their knowledge or consent.

A medical technician at one hospital, who had been incarcerated for raping children, stole a "protected" password and downloaded the confidential records of 954 patients, mostly young women and girls.

Just as anthropologists reconstruct ancient civilizations from the debris left behind, Dumpster divers can surveil your everyday life, reconstruct your personal and financial history—and invade your privacy. Articles found in your trash—condom wrappers, containers for birth control pills, steamy love letters—speak volumes, rightly or wrongly, about your sex life. Discarded prescription bottles can identify many of your medical problems. "Guarding Your Garbage" will show how criminals turn trash into cash, garbage into gold.

Of all the freedoms Americans most cherish, privacy consistently tops the list. But the right to privacy as we know it is currently being attacked on all fronts. *Invasion of Privacy* will increase your awareness of the problem and give you the weapons to fight back.

INVASION

OF

PRIVACY

1

SECRET VIDEOTAPING

J ust imagine you are using a public bathroom, showering at an upscale health club, changing clothes at
a friend's house, or passionately making love with a
trusted partner—and a concealed camera with a zoom
lens is recording your every move. Just imagine, because you could be one of more than twenty thousand
women, men, and children who are unknowingly taped
every day in the United States during their most private
moments. Secret videotaping is the single greatest
threat to personal privacy.

Punch "secret videotaping" into my computer database, press Print, and *thousands* of documented cases
fall to the floor. These are instances in which the victims
had every right to expect privacy.

In a small southern town where churches outnum-
ber bars, more than eighty women were secretly taped
as they suntanned naked at a tanning salon. Even
though the sheriff's daughter and the prosecutor's wife
and daughter were among the victims, no arrests were
made. They couldn't find a state law applicable to this
situation. What investigators did find was a camera behind a two-way mirror in the upper corner of the tan-

ning room. The proprietor reportedly operated the hidden camera by remote control from the front counter. Whether or not the proprietor was tarred and feathered, no one would tell me.

Most people are surprised to learn that the perpetrators of surreptitious surveillances include politicians, movie stars, lawyers, doctors, teachers, business executives, police officers, and members of the clergy.

On May 4, 1996, a pastor in Michigan was arraigned on charges of videotaping female parishioners in the church lavatory and in the bathrooms of two private homes. In Florida, John Giangrossi, a Disney wardrobe assistant, was sentenced to four years of probation for secretly videotaping female performers changing clothes at Walt Disney World. Giangrossi taped the women while hiding in a dumbwaiter near the dressing rooms in Cinderella's Castle. And in Hudson, Wisconsin, a city council member and his wife pleaded guilty to secretly videotaping foreign exchange students as they showered in the couple's home. Interestingly, Don G. Fuller, the forty-two-year-old city council member and his wife, Antoinette, forty, are one of many couples to participate in illegal taping in recent years.

Fuller told the court that he cut a hole through the wall of his bedroom and installed a vent so that he could "videotape the girls taking showers, getting in and getting out, and drying off." Mrs. Fuller admitted that she was aware of the tapings.

The Fullers had graciously hosted a number of foreign students through programs sponsored by the University of Wisconsin and River Falls High School.

A repugnant, highly offensive invasion of privacy,

secret videotaping is occurring in private homes, high schools and colleges, hotels, department store dressing rooms, hospitals, and in offices and workplaces in all fifty states. Thousands of these degrading tapes of innocent and unsuspecting citizens are duplicated and distributed worldwide. Many are even advertised for sale on the Internet.

As part of his assignment with the Bureau of Investigative Services, an unnamed Massachusetts state trooper surfed the Internet in search of illegal activity. During July 1996, the trooper was exploring the Internet when he stumbled upon an advertisement for voyeur videos. Using the title "I See U, U Don't See Me," Robert Novello was selling eight tapes that showed women as they showered, used the bathroom, and changed clothes in health club locker rooms and public rest rooms.

Setting up a sting operation, the state trooper E-mailed Novello and requested a detailed description of the tapes. Novello allegedly replied that the scenes showed women dressing and undressing but focused most attention on women using the toilet.

Using an alias, the trooper purchased one eighty-minute video for $26. Part of the tape showed women as they showered and dried off in a campground shower room. Another part of the tape showed women undressing and showering in a health club locker room. The women were filmed with a camera concealed in the ceiling of the shower room.

Stating that "these videos are an outrageous invasion of privacy," Attorney General Scott Harshbarger temporarily banned Novello Associates from selling the tapes while his office considered legal action. Quoted in the *Boston Globe*, Assistant Attorney General Kevin M. Nasca condemned Novello for "making money off the tapes that violate the privacy of the women on the tapes."

Since investigators could not prove that Novello ordered or participated in the taping and could not identify the victims, there were no criminal charges.

SPYING ON SEX

In 1985, a girl we'll call Liz, a pretty nineteen-year-old, was in love with a boy, a fellow university student we'll call Mark. When Mark invited Liz to make love with him at the parents' home of a friend, Liz, who probably longed for some private time with her boyfriend, smiled gorgeously and accepted the invitation.

Unbeknownst to her, Mark and his buddies had hidden a camera in a closet across from the bed. The unblinking camera recorded every minute of the lovemaking. Knowing the location of the camera and that the tape would be shown to people he hoped to impress, it is probable that Mark maneuvered Liz into the most compromising and embarrassing positions.

As with many other victims of sexual spying, Liz eventually learned through the campus grapevine that the tape was being shown at Mark's fraternity house. Hooting and hollering fraternity boys played and replayed the tape, complete with lewd commentary and play-by-play analyses of Liz's sexual performance.

Feeling betrayed and humiliated, Liz filed suit against Mark and his friends and after a long, difficult legal battle, was awarded $1 million by a jury. Mark appealed the decision, generating yet another legal confrontation. Even though the court ordered that the tape be sealed, the law firm representing Mark defied the order and made two copies. Members of the predominately male law firm were caught watching the tape in a conference room. The firm reportedly paid Liz $650,000 to settle her claim that her privacy had once again been invaded. But the legal battles were not over.

In 1993, the state's highest court reversed lower courts and ruled that Liz was not entitled to damages for mental anguish stemming from the videotape that was secretly made in 1985 and shown to others without her permission.

One of the justices agreed that Liz was the victim of "grossly offensive conduct" but added that her lawyers made the mistake of suing for "negligently inflicted emotional distress" because they apparently hoped to collect damages under homeowners' insurance policies that cover only accidents or careless conduct, not intentional acts.

Needless to say, many women were furious with the reversal and accused the state supreme court of extreme sexism.

Liz could pursue a new legal claim but, exhausted and discouraged, she has indicated that she will not retry the suit.

Betraying the most intimate trust, there are literally hundreds of known—and we assume a much larger number of unknown—instances in which men (usually) have secretly videotaped lovemaking. In many cases, the unwitting victim is the last to know that a tape of her lovemaking has been distributed, repeatedly copied, and viewed by scores of strangers.

Most colleges and universities have implemented training programs for incoming students on such issues as sexual harassment and date rape. Since so many college women have been violated by secret videotaping, it is now time to update codes of conduct and provide mandatory training in ethics and privacy on college campuses.

A nineteen-year-old Massachusetts woman who was unknowingly taped having sex with a fellow university student signed a legal statement in 1996 saying, "My trust was broken in the worst way possible by someone I cared about. . . . There are times when I wish I could crawl under a rock and die."

It was a setup from the beginning. The nineteen-year-old student who had sex with the woman and his immature partner in crime, a twenty-one-year-old resident assistant, concealed the camera in a dorm room. As their targeted victim innocently combed her hair and prepared for her date, the two male students probably joshed and jostled one another and discussed the fun they would have at the woman's expense, treating the woman like a nonperson. It is not hard to imagine the two male students debating which camera angle would be the most titillating and degrading. Perhaps they tested the audio so that even her whispers could be heard.

The two men were expelled from school and placed

on probation for one year, a slap on the wrist. If they don't commit any crimes during the year, all charges will be erased from their records as if the incident never happened. The woman, however, was not so lucky. She will never be able to erase the incident; her sentence is for life.

Dubbed "sex, lies, and videocop" by the press, a case involving a New England police officer proves that spying on sex cannot be dismissed as just an immature college prank and is often committed by someone who should know better. Treating sex like a spectator sport, the officer, like so many other men, secretly filmed more than one partner.

It all began when the officer's live-in girlfriend, the daughter of another police officer, played the tapes she found in his house. The tapes, complete with X-rated audio, showed her policeman boyfriend having sex with two other girlfriends on separate occasions. The girlfriend turned the tapes over to her father, a police sergeant.

Investigators discovered that the officer had offered to show the tapes to another police officer, and they learned that neither of the women depicted on the tapes had any knowledge that they had been filmed. Described as being in their late twenties to early thirties, the women were naturally angry and embarrassed by the discovery. "They certainly did not consent and never would have consented," said the assistant district attorney handling the case.

"That tape is a degrading invasion of privacy and an insult to all women," said a local housewife. "I'd hate to need the police and have that creep show up."

"The sad thing here is that a lot of people think we are not victims and are the ones to blame because we had sex with the guy in his apartment," one of the videotaped women told a major newspaper. "We were violated and our reputations are trashed."

THE RAPE TAPES

"It's like being violated twice," said a thirty-three-year-old nurse who was raped and videotaped. "He not only raped me, he violated my privacy forever by taping it."

Although the horrible incident occurred in 1991, just talking about it in 1997 brought tears to the nurse's eyes. Her voice now trembling and barely audible, she continued, "And damn it, we don't know how many copies are still out there." This mother of two little girls sat and shared her ordeal with me, her arms crossed tightly across her chest and her body slumped into the fetal position.

Unfortunately, the nurse's story is not an isolated case. So many women have been raped and taped in recent years it is beginning to look like a trend.

There have been at least five such cases in Michigan alone and many more in Pennsylvania, New York, California, Connecticut, New Jersey, South Carolina, and several other states. As the Michigan incidents indicate, many of the victims and the perpetrators of so-called tape rapes have been high school and college students.

In 1994, two boys, both seventeen, were convicted of

plying a fourteen-year-old Michigan girl with alcohol and drugs and then videotaping sex acts with her. That same year, police in Michigan, accused a nineteen-year-old with videotaping himself having sex with an unconscious thirteen-year-old girl. Then in 1995, again in Michigan, three teenage boys were convicted of a videotaped sexual assault on a thirteen-year-old girl.

The videotaped incident that occurred at a Michigan university in 1996 is typical of incidents that have occurred in a dozen other states. Increasingly, the rape victims are unconscious or incapacitated during the assault.

"Did you know there is a tape of you being passed around campus?" a concerned student told the eighteen-year-old freshman. "No!" the surprised girl reportedly answered. Blushing with embarrassment, the concerned student then explained that the tape showed five basketball players having sex with her. "What!?" the horrified student probably responded.

In truth, the traumatized girl had no recollection of what happened after she attended a college holiday party. She passed out after drinking at the off-campus apartment where the party was held and woke up the next morning suffering from mysterious injuries.

But a Michigan state prosecutor who was quoted by the Associated Press believes he knows exactly what happened. He saw the tape.

According to the prosecutor, the tape, seized from one of the athletes, clearly identifies the attackers and reportedly shows that the sex acts were not consensual. The woman was drunk or possibly drugged and was apparently helpless.

"There's no part of that tape that is not graphic," he said. "It's awful."

Rape is awful. But to be videotaped while being raped, as the nurse described, is to be violated twice.

CAMERAS IN THE HOME

In Fort Collins, Colorado, a prominent forty-four-year-old eye doctor was charged with videotaping dozens of people using the bathroom and the guest room in his home.

Dr. Richard Hammond turned himself in to police after a woman who was house-sitting at his home found a camera hidden in a basement bathroom. Authorities discovered that there were actually two cameras mounted and concealed in the bathroom and found seven VCRs, which were set up to record from the cameras. The cameras started automatically when the bathroom light was turned on. A hidden camera was also discovered in a guest room.

Since many of the secretly videotaped victims included friends of his thirteen-year-old daughter, Dr. Hammond was also charged with sexual exploitation of children.

Needing time to review the more than three hundred confiscated tapes, prosecutors were granted a ten-day delay in filing charges. Free on his own recognizance, Dr. Hammond checked into a Denver hotel on March 25, 1995, and used a heavy dose of sodium cyanide to commit suicide.

Despite the death of Dr. Hammond, police were obligated to continue their investigation and to determine if the tapes—and the privacy of scores of citizens—had been sold on the open market. There was also mounting pressure from over one hundred friends, relatives, neighbors, and coworkers to determine if their most private moments had been taped.

It is estimated that over three hundred thousand crimes are committed in the United States each year by criminals who have somehow obtained keys to private homes, apartments, offices, cars, and so forth. These same keys, which are primarily used for home invasions, are increasingly being used to invade our privacy. Many times, there is no state law to protect us.

During August 1994, a couple in Maryland went on vacation and, as was their custom, gave a key to their neighbor so he could keep an eye on their house. When the couple returned from their vacation, they thanked the neighbor profusely for his help and went about their lives.

Then, in January 1995, the couple was adjusting a heating vent in their bathroom when they discovered a camera. Later that night, the couple found a second camera behind a heating vent in a dressing room and followed cables leading through their attic, down a drain pipe, and underground into their neighbor's home. The neighbor had been watching the couple in the bathroom and the dressing room for months—and it wasn't against the law.

"It was like being raped," the offended woman told the Maryland House Judiciary Committee. "I was being stalked. And the worst part of it is, it was my own home."

The couple addressed state legislators in hopes that they would pass laws making it illegal to place video cameras in private homes and other private places without the permission of the persons being filmed. Maryland law currently states only that it is illegal to place a video camera in retail store dressing rooms and bathrooms. "Big deal!" said a Maryland woman who was once spied on while using the bathroom in a shopping center. "Even if the video voyeur is caught, it's only a slap-on-the-wrist misdemeanor."

Although the neighbor admitted placing the cameras and confessed that he was obsessed with the wife, he was never arrested. The couple is trying to file a civil suit against him. In the meantime, the man who watched them on the toilet, in the shower, and getting dressed and undressed for six months is still their neighbor.

When cameras are discovered in private homes, much to the horror of the occupants, police will usually interview the landlord of the property. And with good reason. The landlord had total access to the dwelling before it was occupied, knows others who gained entrance in the past, and continues to have access once the residents move in. I have been informed of twenty-seven cases in thirteen states in which landlords concealed cameras to invade the privacy of their tenants. It is assumed that these twenty-seven cases represent only a small fraction of the total number.

When caught, most landlords offered outrageous excuses for their voyeurism. Police arrested a landlord in New York in 1996 and charged him with spying on a couple who were renting his basement apartment.

While dressing one night, the woman noticed a light emanating from the back of the full-length mirror in the bedroom. When her male friend investigated, he found it was a two-way mirror with a hole behind it. He immediately called police, who discovered a video camera on a tripod in a closet adjacent to the couples' bedroom. The equipment was focused on the tenant's bed.

The landlord told police he used the sophisticated camera to make sure the couple didn't smoke in the house.

Sparing no expense, several landlords have purchased the very best equipment and spied on a succession of tenants before being caught.

On May 17, 1996, the Indiana Supreme Court suspended attorney John M. Haecker for secretly videotaping a succession of tenants, who were often naked, in the duplex he rented to them. "His acts bring into question his fitness as one who can be trusted to keep his clients' secrets or give effective legal advice," the Indiana court concluded.

Investigators discovered that Haecker wired the house with three video cameras so he could spy on his tenants from the adjoining side. The three cameras were aimed at the toilet, the bed, and the shower.

While showering, a female tenant noticed a hole in the ceiling. She and her male companion then found the cameras with wires leading to Haecker's side of the duplex.

Searching Haecker's home, investigators discovered a treasure trove of video equipment including two videocassette recorders, a digital video mixer, a video camera, a pinhole camera, and a miniature microphone.

Indiana's Supreme Court stated the obvious: "Our gravest concern is that the respondent's actions were the product of a deliberate, premeditated plan to invade the privacy of the occupants of his rental property."

The incident motivated the General Assembly to pass a 1995 law making voyeurism a Class D felony punishable by up to three years in prison when the crime involves a videotape. Before that, it was only considered a misdemeanor with a maximum six-month sentence.

SURVEILLANCE IN THE WORKPLACE

When a teenage Maryland resident we'll call Leslie Richards reported to work as a lifeguard at a public swimming pool in Maryland in 1992, she had every right to expect total privacy as she changed from her street clothes to her swimsuit. But a video camera in the employee dressing room, concealed by her male supervisor denied her this right. Instead of privacy and respect for a job well done, the energetic employee received public humiliation.

Richards didn't know about the tape until she heard about it from other staff members. She would later learn that her college-aged supervisor had hidden the camera beneath a pile of dirty clothes in a laundry basket and had shown the tape to at least five other men. Feeling degraded, Richards quit the job she loved at the pool.

Fortunately, one man was indeed an honest man and refused to be part of the spectators. One of the other pool employees would later testify that Richards's supervisor took him to the first aid room and showed him, through the viewfinder of a video camcorder, a videotape of Richards changing clothes. "I turned it off and told him that what he had done was wrong and that he should destroy it."

Privacy denied, Richards sought justice. "I was extremely embarrassed when I first heard about it. People say things," Richards told the court on August 16, 1993. An hour later, the judge found the supervisor guilty of secret videotaping and sentenced him to thirty days in jail, with all but five days suspended, and fined him a whopping $100.

"That's all he got!" said a thirty-year-old haberdasher. "Maybe I'll sneak a camera into the women's dressing rooms at work," he joked. If he expected a laugh from his girlfriend, he didn't get it. She gave him a look of disgust, yanked his arm from her waist, and abruptly distanced herself from him. "What's the matter?" he yelled as she walked away.

But justice, too, would be denied. The conviction in state District Court was overturned when a Circuit Court judge agreed that the Maryland statute that forbids secret videotaping applies only to changing rooms in stores, not dressing rooms at swimming pools or other locations.

Richards won in civil court. On December 8, 1995, a federal jury ordered Montgomery County to pay her $140,000. The supervisor had earlier agreed to pay her $24,000 to settle her lawsuit against him.

Testimony at the civil trials revealed that male recreation department staff members spied on hundreds of other women and girls through a peephole to the women's locker room in early 1993. When the director of the aquatic center learned of the peephole, he had it filled with spackling compound. When that was found chipped away three days later, he ordered the hole filled with concrete.

Despite six months of peeping by who knows how many men, there was never an investigation. Richards's attorney would later cite this as evidence that the pool was run as a boys' club.

Most workers now accept or at least tolerate security cameras in the public areas of the workplace. While they may not welcome this intrusion into their privacy, they understand that shoplifting, theft, and other crimes dictate the need for some form of surveillance. But these same workers are becoming increasingly angry with authorized and unauthorized spying in such private areas as bathrooms and locker rooms.

Offering flimsy excuses for secret videotaping, many employers create a huge problem when they try to solve a minor one.

"Someone was apparently stealing toilet paper from the ladies' rest room," explained the female office manager of a multinational corporation headquartered in New York. "So the idiots installed a hidden camera directly over the toilet stalls. . . . We were furious."

The incident, which was settled out of court, only came to light because a female security guard mentioned to the office manager that she would never use that rest room.

"Those creeps had been watching us change tampons and using the toilet for six months because they wanted to find a toilet paper thief. . . . Oh, please! God, it was so humiliating."

Trying to find humor in a horrible situation, the forty-eight-year-old woman concluded that "losing $30 in toilet paper would have been a lot, lot cheaper than the money they had to pay us.

"Lou, when I saw the closeup of myself using the toilet, I just wanted to die. None of us could believe that this would happen in America."

Many workers have discovered that tapes allegedly used for security reasons have been exploited for other purposes.

In 1993 a JCPenney employee learned that an immature department store security guard was showing a tape he made of her. Using the store's ceiling cameras, the guard zoomed in on her breasts. "Enough to give any woman the creeps," her attorney told the media. The case was settled out of court.

The presence of security cameras in the workplace is currently accomplishing more good than bad. In St. Joseph, Missouri, a surveillance camera caught a disgruntled employee urinating in an office coffeepot. In Orlando, Florida, a hidden camera filmed hotel maids stealing guests' wallets and selling master keys to criminals. And in at least forty-six states, secret videotaping has recorded employees selling and using illegal drugs. Hundreds of thousands of workplace crimes including theft, armed robbery, and murder have been captured on tape.

The bad news is that as Big Brother gets bigger and

the cameras get smaller, there will be less and less privacy in the workplace. Striking a balance between our right to privacy and our right to a safe work environment, executives will have to think before installing a camera, respect private areas like rest rooms, and make sure that the cameras do not cause more harm than good.

During the last decade, there have been more than two thousand serious abuses of video cameras in the workplace. A short sampling of these cases follows.

1991—Illinois: A union representing employees at an Amoco Corporation plant filed a lawsuit against the company for installing a hidden camera in the women's shower room. Company officials said the camera had been installed to catch a man who had been sneaking in. At least one female employee believed she had been taped in the nude. Asking for $10 million in damages, the union contended that the company illegally invaded the privacy of female employees.

1992—Virginia: A nurse at the Southside Regional Medical Center in Petersburg discovered a camera in a women's locker room. Hospital administrators said that the surveillance camera was put in the private area to stop vandalism.

1992—California: Employees who sued over a surveillance camera concealed in a San Francisco police station bathroom failed to prove a policy of spying. The police chief had authorized installation of the camera to find out who clogged the urinal several times with toilet paper.

1993—Massachusetts: Employees at Boston's Sheraton Hotel sued for invasion of privacy when they discovered that a tiny camera was monitoring their every move while they dressed and undressed in a locker room. One waiter was filmed with nothing on but his jockstrap. Sheraton installed the camera as part of an investigation into suspected drug use by its workers.

1994—Virginia: Thomas A. Dietrich, thirty-one, a former salesman at Luskins electronic store, pleaded guilty to sexually molesting young girls in the store—and videotaping himself doing it—while their unknowing parents shopped nearby. Dietrich used the store video equipment and taped himself pulling down the girls' underwear and fondling them. His wife found the horrible tapes in their home and handed them over to the police. Fairfax City police were able to identify six of the ten victims on the tapes.

1995—New York: A male X-ray technician at a large New York City hospital was accused of videotaping a patient while she was undressed. The technician made an unauthorized appointment for a woman to come to the radiology lab at a time when the lab was closed. When the patient arrived, the technician allegedly told her to disrobe and put a lubricant on her breasts. The patient reported that the employee videotaped her while she was doing this.

SCHOOLS AND COLLEGES

While attending a baseball game at a southern high school nine girls ages ten to fourteen entered the school in search of a bathroom. The popular middle-aged sports director at the school, greeted the girls in his usual friendly manner and escorted them down the hallway to a faculty rest room that was normally not intended for students' use. As the girls used the facilities, one of them discovered a video camera concealed in a cardboard box. They later reported that the box was angled in such a way that the hidden camera captured their bodies only from the shoulders down.

"I'm sitting here worrying that there are films of my daughter going to the bathroom plastered all over the Internet," the father of one of the girls said in a media account. "You have to wonder just how long this has been going on."

Police searches of the sports director's home and offices at the high school turned up more than 110 video-tapes and four video cameras.

On December 9, 1996, the sports director pleaded no contest to attempting to videotape a girl while she used a school rest room. In exchange for the plea and his resignation from the school, prosecutors agreed not to pursue three felony charges against him. Had he been convicted of all three counts, the educator could have been sentenced to thirty-one years in prison.

From January 1990 to January 1997, at least 1,835 students and staff members are known to have been illegally and secretly videotaped in the educational environment. These secret videotapings, which almost always involved some degree of nudity, were committed by students or staff members at schools or colleges in the United States. They included appalling cases in which educators improperly filmed students and incidents in which students improperly filmed other students, on and off campus. A high percentage of the incidents involved sexually oriented filming of elementary and junior high school students. Since many voyeurs tape scores of victims before they are caught (and many others are never caught), the actual number of illegally taped victims in the educational environment may very well be in the tens of thousands. The reader should also be aware that there are many cases in which secret videotaping is highly suspected but not proven. Suspected incidents were excluded from our research.

Some video spying cases originated at off-campus locations but ended up being exploited on school property. In one such case, a school board in California expelled a seventeen-year-old high school athlete for secretly videotaping himself and a fourteen-year-old girl having sex and showing the tape at school on a screen attached to a camcorder. The fourteen-year-old girl—and her parents—were naturally mortified when they learned what the boy had done.

An example of an off-campus case involving a high school principal occurred in 1996 in the Midwest.

A principal in a local high school was suspended without pay while police investigated allegations that he secretly videotaped twelve cheerleaders while they undressed and put on swimsuits for a beach party at his lakefront home.

The cheerleaders told police that they were changing into bathing suits when they noticed a flashing red light behind a bathroom mirror, then observed that the light was coming from a video camera.

When police obtained a search warrant for the principal's home, they seized a smoked-glass mirror, a trapdoor, and thirty-four tapes that allegedly showed the school's varsity cheerleaders changing clothes for the swim party.

Most of the secret videotaping cases my staff and I reviewed occurred at on-campus locations in such areas as rest rooms, locker rooms, and fraternity houses.

On September 23, 1996, two male university students, ages twenty and twenty-one, were accused of videotaping a woman having sex in their fraternity house. The female student told police that she was making love with one of the men in a room at their fraternity house when she discovered a second man who was hiding in the closet and videotaping them.

Several people in recent years have been caught secretly filming high school girls in school locker rooms. The video voyeurs have included a janitor in Alaska and a track coach in Virginia.

Secret videotaping at schools and colleges is a widespread, ever-growing problem that has received very little attention. Existing data on this subject suggests that it is time to wake up and start demanding our right to privacy.

PROTECTING OUR PRIVACY

◆ Secret videotaping may very well be the single greatest threat to personal privacy. More than 20,000 women, men, and children are unknowingly taped every day in situations where the expectation and the right to privacy should be guaranteed, i.e., while showering, dressing, using a public rest room, or making love in their own homes. We should be willing to make some compromises in the interest of security and safety, but when secret videotaping becomes a highly offensive intrusion into our privacy, we need to vigorously fight for our rights.

◆ We've been caught with our legal pants down. Existing laws need to be amended and updated to catch up with the growing problem of secret videotaping. When a neighbor set up cameras in a Maryland couples' shower and bedroom, there were no laws to protect the couple. When an Indiana landlord pointed secret cameras at his tenant's bed, toilet, and shower, the incident was treated as a misdemeanor. Many people who have been videotaped in locker rooms have had no legal recourse because the laws

against videotaping applied only to store dressing rooms. This is insane. Pressure legislators
to pass laws that will forbid secret videotaping
in homes, bedrooms, showers, rest rooms, and
locker rooms. Voyeurism with a video camera
in a private area should be upgraded to a
felony punishable with a very stiff penalty.

♦ Report rumors of peeping and secret videotaping (in rest rooms, locker rooms, private
homes, and fraternity houses) to the proper
authorities and refuse to participate, no matter
how titillating, in this offensive behavior. Notify
victims if you know that a private tape is being
circulated. In one case, seven "friends" of a female victim failed to notify her that her "boyfriend" was circulating a secretly made tape of
their lovemaking. The victim learned of the
tape after copies were widely distributed. "I felt
betrayed by my boyfriend *and* my girlfriends
who didn't help me."

♦ Totally hidden video? Not always. Concealed
video cameras are often easy to find. Cameras
are frequently hidden behind two-way mirrors,
in heating vents, or concealed in a closet or
some innocuous container such as a box, gym
bag, or laundry hamper. I know of eight cameras that were discovered when residents saw a
light behind their mirror. Worried about a
neighbor who was obsessed with his daughter,
one man disassembled a full-length mirror in

his daughter's apartment and discovered a penny-sized hole leading to the stalker's apartment. At least six cameras have been discovered when victims grew suspicious of odd clicks, rewinding sounds, and other electrically generated noises. Being cautious or suspicious doesn't make you paranoid. A camera was discovered in a health club shower when one member questioned why a woman always seemed to be taking showers and always brought a gym bag into the shower room. Thinking that there was a medicine cabinet behind the mirror in her hotel bathroom, a female bank executive gave it a tug. To her horror, the mirror came off and exposed a camera. Many cameras can film through the tiniest of holes. When searching for a hidden camera, don't forget the ceiling and the floors; voyeurs often utilize the crawl spaces for hidden cameras. Be most suspicious of walls that adjoin other residences.

♦ Some concealment tactics are very sophisticated. Sometimes you watch television and sometimes the television watches you. At least three companies make television sets that conceal video cameras. The camera will work if the television is on or off and can be triggered to begin taping by movement or sound. Some companies have installed these television cameras in lunch rooms. Interestingly, the same companies that made the TV camera also advertise a Video Camera Detector. Video cameras used to spy on baby-sitters, criminals, and people making love in the privacy of their homes have also been concealed in computers, stereos, smoke detectors, clocks, and childrens' dolls and toys. Be aware of the Trojan horse tactic. If an unsavory character wanted to spy on you, he might give you a gift containing a camera or a listening device. Remember, too, many secret cameras are mobile. Mini–video cameras, some the size of a lipstick canister, can be hidden in a voyeur's baseball hat or in a woman's hair. These are the cameras frequently used by investigative reporters.

♦ If you discover a hidden video camera, don't stand in front of it talking about it. Try to act as normal as possible so that the perpetrator, if watching the tape, does not realize you have discovered the camera. You don't want the voyeur to destroy all the evidence (as has happened several times) before the police get a search warrant. If you believe your own telephone might be in view of the camera, notify police as soon as possible from a pay phone. It might be unwise to borrow a nearby neighbor's telephone, especially if you live in an attached town house, apartment, or group house; the neighbor might be the perpetrator.

♦ Employers should think before authorizing a secret surveillance camera. Is it right to install a camera over a toilet stall in hopes of capturing a toilet paper thief? Will the camera create a huge problem out of a small problem? Will the bad outweigh the good? Does the camera symbolize a lack of respect for the employees? Will the tape be an insult to human dignity and adversely affect morale? Employers should ask themselves: "Would I feel humiliated or offended being taped in this situation?" "Would I want my family to be subject to such a surveillance?" Is the camera going to get the company sued? Is there an ulterior motive for the taping? Employers have a responsibility to insure that the tape is not inappropriately exploited.

♦ Employers, schools, and colleges need to educate employees and students about the importance of respecting privacy and warn them that secret videotaping is considered a serious, repugnant offense. Codes of conduct should now include sections on date rape, sexual harassment, and secret videotaping.

♦ Be aware of the tricks and deceptive techniques many video voyeurs have used in the past. You dramatically increase the chances of being victimized if you consume drugs or alcohol or allow yourself to be isolated with a group or an individual you don't know and trust. Posing for unknown photographers, casting directors, and modeling agents can be very risky. Several women who modeled swimsuits discovered they were secretly videotaped in the changing rooms. A hospital technician in New York City told a woman he could provide free X rays, but she would have to come to his office after work. The woman was secretly videotaped when she disrobed. A woman who was offered private karate lessons in a man's home was secretly filmed when she changed clothes.

♦ Police, lawyers, and security personnel should handle confiscated tapes in a sensitive and professional manner in order to respect the privacy and dignity of the victims. Only people directly involved with the case, with an absolute need to know, should view tapes that are embarrassing to the victim. Tapes should be secured so that there is no possibility they will be stolen, lost, copied, or viewed by unauthorized personnel. Lewd comments, jokes, and wisecracks concerning the tapes are totally unacceptable. Immature and gossip-prone personnel have no business being involved in sensitive secret videotaping cases. A law firm was successfully sued for $650,000 when several partners were caught viewing a steamy tape the judge had ordered sealed.

♦ Warning: As video cameras become more popular, many consenting adults are choosing to make private X-rated tapes of themselves. This is their own business. Be advised, however, that in literally thousands of known cases, these videos have come back to haunt the people who made them. Sometimes the tapes are lost or stolen and sometimes they get mixed up with other, less compromising tapes. Some have accidently been placed in the wrong carton and returned to a video store. More commonly, the participants break up, and one partner uses the tape for blackmail or to entertain friends.

2

WHO'S LISTENING TO YOUR CELLULAR AND CORDLESS PHONE CALLS?

More than forty million cellular phones are currently in use in the United States, and the numbers are dramatically increasing each year.

On any given day, thousands of eavesdroppers intercept, record, and listen to conversations made from cellular and so-called cordless phones. These eavesdroppers include curious neighbors, business competitors, stalkers, journalists, private investigators, and even espionage agents.

In California, spies for hire cruise the highways of Hollywood and the Silicon Valley, hoping to steal valuable trade secrets from executives talking on their car phones. Armed with radio scanners, tabloid reporters in New York monitor conversations of the rich, famous, and infamous, hoping to get a front-page scoop. In Florida, a ham operator monitoring the poolside conversations of a prominent lawyer got incredible inside information on three divorce cases.

Cellular telephone conversations can be easily monitored by anyone with a radio scanner, but it is a violation of state and federal law to do so intentionally. A 1993 law made it illegal to make or sell radio scanners that pick up cellular calls, but the law didn't make it illegal to own the old scanners. Furthermore, it is rather easy, although illegal, to modify a legal police scanner so that it will pick up cellular conversations.

The problem is that there are hundreds of thousands of the old radio scanners in circulation and an equal number of people who don't care about the law. "How are they going to catch me and how are they going to prove it?" said one ham operator who listens to his neighbors' cellular conversations "just for the fun of it."

In truth, only a very small percentage of the people who have been monitored ever learn that their calls were intercepted. An even smaller percentage of the perpetrators are ever caught. Curious kooks, corporate snoops, and spies for hire who use intercepted information are usually smart enough not to publicize where they got it.

"I really couldn't care less if someone listens to my conversations," said a schoolteacher from Indiana. "I'm not discussing my love life or national security." One of the biggest problems concerning privacy and portable phones is that most people do not realize how even innocent information can be used by criminals and other opportunists. Another problem is that just because you don't care if someone is listening to your conversation, the person you are talking to might care very much.

Burglars are known to monitor the calls of people discussing evening or weekend plans. Knowing that the occupants are going to be away, the burglars enter their homes.

Doctors and lawyers frequently discuss everyday business on cellular phones. In one case, a doctor was notified that a VIP patient had tested positive for AIDS. The information was intercepted, and before long, the VIP's medical status was common knowledge. In another case, a lawyer from Ohio reviewed a client's prenuptial agreement with a second lawyer who was using a cellular telephone. A teenage neighbor of the second lawyer intercepted the conversation. "Before long, the whole damn neighborhood knew about our secret wedding and my financial situation," said the angry groom-to-be.

Stalking, or inappropriate pursuit, has become a dangerous epidemic in the United States and is evolving into one of the most insidious threats to personal privacy. Many researchers estimate that more than two hundred thousand women, men, and children are currently being harassed, threatened, and endangered by stalkers.

Stalking may begin with an innocuous contact and then, through misinterpretation or delusion, the pursuer escalates to harassment, surveillance, threats, and sometimes murder.

I have been involved in seven cases and am aware of many more in which stalkers intercepted cellular phone conversations and used the intelligence to harass their targets.

A jobless and toothless forty-one-year-old man, hooked on amphetamines, became infatuated with a fifteen-year-old girl whom he first noticed at a state swimming competition. "He's really scary and keeps showing up wherever I go," explained the frightened swimmer. "It's like he always knows where I'm going to be."

The young lady had good reason to be scared; the man had a long history of bizarre and criminal behavior. On one occasion, he burglarized a home and fell asleep in a teenage girl's bed. The horrified family called the police who arrested the man and confiscated handcuffs and a number of stolen house keys.

Released on good behavior, the "nonviolent" criminal was once again free to victimize others. We can't prove what his ultimate plans were concerning our fifteen-year-old client, but we did prove that he had a scanner in his car and had recorded the swimmer's mother as she talked on various cell phones, including a car phone. Two of the taped conversations informed the stalker where his target would be. "I've got to pick my daughter up at McDonald's at 4:30," she mentioned to one friend. "The swim team is celebrating at the Hyatt tonight," she told her neighbor. Needless to say, the stalker showed up at both locations.

Eavesdropping on cellular phones is only one of the issues that worry privacy advocates. There is also concern that cellular phones will be used by police and sophisticated criminals to locate the caller.

Unbeknownst to most consumers, cellular phones are portable homing devices that allow police and others to pinpoint the caller's position. Police have used this tool to locate a wide range of criminals and kidnap victims. Privacy advocates worry that police will abuse this tool to spy on innocent citizens.

When a cellular phone is switched to the On position, it emits a low-power signal to the network to announce which cell site it is in. A cell site is a zone served by a single relay station and is generally several square miles in size. When a caller moves out of one cell site, the call is automatically switched to a different cell site.

By using a technique called triangulation, police are able to get a directional fix on the cellular signal and pinpoint the phone's cell site or location. This is the technique police used to locate the car owned by the slain father of basketball great Michael Jordan. Triangulation techniques have also been used by intelligence agencies to locate enemy radio sites and by ocean search-and-rescue teams to pinpoint the location of vessels.

There are dozens of cases in which triangulation techniques have assisted law enforcement worldwide.

When the Los Angeles police needed to locate O. J. Simpson during the now-famous highway chase, they received court-ordered help from a mobile phone company and were able to locate the Ford Bronco by tracing its cellular phone radio signal. In Colombia, ruthless drug boss Pablo Escobar was finally located and shot dead by police after they traced his mobile telephone's radio signal. Police in the United States located fugitive lawyer Nicholas Bissell, Jr., in Nevada on November 26, 1996, after tracing calls he made on his cellular telephone. Bissell was running from the law after being convicted of fraud, embezzlement, and abuse of power.

Another advantage of cellular tracing from a law enforcement perspective is that cellular phones can tell police not only where a suspect is going but also where he has been.

A federal drug informant is accused of booby-trapping a briefcase in an unsuccessful attempt to kill a U. S. prosecutor. Using the informant's cellular phone records, prosecutors showed that he was in the same town on the same day where the would-be assassination kit was purchased.

Unlike hard-line telephones that most people have in their homes, customers pay for each local cellular call. The billing record for each cellular call shows the cell site from which it was made.

Privacy advocates recognize that cellular call tracing can be a great tool for law enforcement, but they argue that the bad will outweigh the good if police abuse their powers.

"Police have no right to know my location just because they reason that I might be relevant to some investigation," explained a law-abiding political science professor. "I want to make sure police cannot track and follow a person using a mobile phone unless they obtain a full wiretap warrant." At present, police only need a simple subpoena, which is easier to obtain than a wiretap warrant, to legally intercept cell phone signals.

"I bet the good professor would change his mind real quickly if his daughter were kidnapped," countered a police captain. "We don't have the time, the resources, or the inclination to snoop on law-abiding citizens. . . . We only use cellular tools to catch criminals," he protested. "Shouldn't we be more worried about the way rapists and burglars invade our privacy and less worried about taking crime-fighting weapons away from the police?"

As the section at the end of this chapter, "Protecting Your Privacy," indicates, there is a great deal that can be done to protect the privacy of mobile phone users, but it is important to balance our right to privacy with our right to be protected from criminals.

CELEBRITY INTERCEPTION

It is estimated that more than four thousand celebrities in the United States, including politicians, movie stars, athletes, and CEOs, have been secretly monitored while using cellular telephones. Most eavesdroppers, however, are never caught or prosecuted. The following incidents illustrate the dangers and embarrassment caused by intercepted calls.

In Jacksonville, Florida, on December 21, 1996, John Martin and his wife, Alice, intercepted a part of history on their handheld police scanner. Speaker Newt Gingrich was holding a conference call with Rep. John A. Boehner of Ohio and other House Republicans. They were discussing the counterattack that should be launched once Gingrich admitted ethical violations. Ironically, Gingrich had promised not to use his office and allies to orchestrate a response to those charges. The conversation was easily intercepted because Rep. Boehner was using a cellular phone in his car.

Britain's Princess Diana and Prince Charles have both had intimate cellular phone calls intercepted. The princess and prince were both talking to lovers when the calls were intercepted, and both paid a very public price for their indiscretion. A seventeen-minute cellular telephone call between Prince Philip, Queen Elizabeth's husband, and an unidentified woman was intercepted and taped in 1996. The prince reportedly moaned about the marital woes of his son Charles.

Robert Wayne "Bobby" Dunnington intercepted a car phone conversation in 1988 in which Lt. Governor L. Douglas Wilder bad-mouthed political rival Chuck Robb. Police found 154 cassette tapes containing numerous recorded calls in Dunnington's home.

While playing golf in 1990, Texas congressman Bill Sarpalius pulled out a cell phone and reportedly made a date with a twenty-year-old woman whom he complemented as being "cute." The conversation was taped by an eavesdropping seventy-five-year-old ham operator. The congressman later explained to *The Washington Post* that he was trying to get a date for a friend, not for himself.

Police arrested two private investigators in Jerusalem after they were caught methodically intercepting the cellular phone calls of Israeli President Ezer Weizman, Tel Aviv Mayor Ronni Milo, and 229 other prominent Israelis. A senior official

stated that many of the conversations were considered politically and personally indiscreet and
highly embarrassing. Although Israel is considered
a security-conscious nation, the PIs had no problem intercepting calls to banks, newspapers, and
the Israeli Defense Ministry.

PROTECTING YOUR PRIVACY

♦ Anyone with the right equipment can listen to
  your cellular and cordless telephone conversations. If you wouldn't say something in a
  crowded elevator, don't say it on an open cell
  phone.

♦ Callers need to inform one another if they are
  using a mobile phone; eavesdroppers can listen in if only one party is talking on a cordless
  or cellular device.

♦ Advanced technology that makes it possible for
  messages to be digitized and encrypted will
  eliminate the effectiveness of analog scanners,
  make it increasingly difficult for outsiders to
  eavesdrop, and will ensure greater privacy. Nevertheless, with new technology being developed almost daily, nothing is undecipherable
  and no telephone will ever be totally private.
  Before purchasing mobile phone equipment,

tell the salesperson you want a phone that offers the maximum amount of security.

♦ Cellular phones can be used as homing devices to pinpoint your location. This can be good and bad. If abducted or lost in a snowstorm, police might be able to locate you if your cell phone is switched On.

♦ It is important to remember that laws forbidding unauthorized interceptions of cellular phones will be ignored by many eavesdroppers.

♦ To listen in for long periods of time, the eavesdropper usually needs to be very close to a stationary cell-phone user. It is difficult to monitor car phones for long periods if the vehicle continues to exit and enter new cell sites. When a caller leaves a cell site, the call is automatically switched to a different cell site, which usually assigns the call to a different radio frequency. This new frequency causes the eavesdropper's scanner to lose the connection.

♦ Remember, your cellular phone bills profile who you have been calling. Hard-line phone bills usually only list the long distance numbers you have called. Cellular phone bills, however, also list the local phone numbers you've called. There are many legitimate reasons why people would not want their local calls known to outsiders. "I didn't want my boss to know I had medical problems," explained one woman who was issued a cellular phone for her work. "But the phone records showed that I called the hospital twice a day."

♦ Warning: Cellular phones can interfere with cardiac pacemakers, interrupting their ability to regulate the heart. Researchers at the Mayo Clinic teamed up with researchers at the University of Oklahoma and Tufts–New England Medical Center in Boston to study the effects of five types of cellular phones on 975 people with pacemakers. The study found that nearly 54 percent of the participants experienced some type of pacemaker interference from cellular phones. In some cases, the phones turned off the pacemaker. In other cases, the phones prompted the heart to speed to an inappropriately fast rate. Researchers discovered that cellular interference is most worrisome for those people who would otherwise have no heart rhythm without their pacemakers. The study indicated that cellular phones pose no risk to bystanders with pacemakers. There is no evidence that cordless phones interfere with pacemakers. The study offered encouraging news on how people with pacemakers could reduce risks associated with cellular phones. People with pacemakers should consult a medical specialist before using a cellular phone.

♦ Drivers chatting on car phones have a greater risk of accidents. Distracted motorists using car phones have reportedly caused thousands of accidents. Motorists who talk on the phone while sipping a drink or lighting a cigarette are even more dangerous. A man paralyzed from the waist down due to a car accident said, "Her right to use that damn car phone has left me crippled for life." Car phones can be a great convenience and an excellent security tool for motorists. It is the responsibility of the cell phone users to make sure their mobile conversations do not endanger themselves or others.

3

STEALING VOICE MAIL

National Regulatory Services Inc., a respected company located in Salisbury, Connecticut, became aware of the problems during September 1995. Executives of the successful company couldn't help but notice that business, for no apparent reason, was beginning to drop off. And then there were the complaints. Loyal, longtime clients were suddenly threatening to take their business elsewhere because their repeated phone messages were not being returned. *What's going on?* the executives must have thought.

The answer turned out to be rather simple. As with dozens of other companies in recent years, a former employee was sabotaging the business by stealing voice mail. In this case, it cost the company an estimated $1 million in business.

Noticing irregularities in its voice mail system, National Regulatory Services Inc. contacted the FBI and the state police. Working with the company, the FBI planted a fake phone message from a legitimate client in National's voice mail service.

The sting worked. State police say that a disgruntled former employee retrieved the client's message, deleted it from National's voice mail system, and then called the client in hopes of stealing the contract.

After his dismissal from National Regulatory Services Inc., the employee went to work for a competitor. The companies help brokers and investment consultants meet regulatory requirements.

Using inside knowledge, the disgruntled employee regularly accessed his former employer's computer mail, listened to business calls, deleted messages, and stole clients.

On February 8, 1996, the former employee was arrested and charged with twenty-nine counts of computer crime, one count of third-degree larceny, and two counts of harassment. He was held on $510,000 bond.

The ever-changing world of computers and telecommunications has given birth to a new type of tele-criminal: the voice mail hacker. Intent on espionage, sabotage, or mischief, voice mail hackers are stealing clients, trade secrets, and reputations.

In 118 known cases, voice mail saboteurs have illegally entered private voice mailboxes and changed friendly greetings to obscene or destructive messages. A radio station was shocked to discover that their public service message was altered to a foul-mouthed tirade. Mimicking a female's voice, a rejected suitor in Washington, D.C., changed a woman's voice mail message to: "Sorry I can't answer your call, but I've been arrested for prostitution." A secretary at a Chicago bank returned to work on Monday and discovered that the friendly, professional greeting she left on Friday had been altered to heavy breathing.

"Since we didn't discover the sabotage for several days, there's no telling how much it cost us," explained the owner of a mail-order business. Someone had entered the company's voice mail system and left a "We are no longer in business" message.

Some enterprising tele-hackers have even used telephone call-forwarding schemes to siphon customers from the competition.

On September 18, 1995, in Bucks County, Pennsylvania, Michael Lasch, a thirty-six-year-old plumber, pleaded guilty to unlawful use of a computer and to stealing customers from five plumbing companies.

Lasch called Bell Atlantic and ordered a service known as Ultra Call Forwarding for telephones listed in the names of rival plumbing companies.

Activating the service from a push-button phone, Lasch intercepted the calls that customers placed to the other plumbers. The five plumbing companies lost tens of thousands of dollars.

Guilty of impersonation, theft by deception, and various forms of tele-fraud and tele-mischief, Lasch was sentenced to seven to twenty-three months in prison.

Alerted to these relatively new telecommunication tactics, companies are instructing employees to change their pass codes on a regular basis and to be on the lookout for irregularities in their voice mail systems.

How often do employers intercept the personal voice mail messages of employees? Very often. Is this legal? Are electronic voice mailboxes granted the same confidentiality protections as live telephone calls or postal mail? The jury is still undecided.

Two individuals we'll call David Johnson and Amy Silver worked at the same fast-food restaurant but in towns sixty miles apart. David and Amy began having a romantic affair in 1993.

Johnson, who had been married for fifteen years and has two children, began working at the restaurant shortly after high school and worked his way up to regional supervisor. Silver was one position below store manager in another of the chain's restaurants when she and Johnson began their affair.

To pass the time between their amorous get-togethers, Johnson and Silver began sending steamy love messages to each other on their voice mail at work.

Much to the shock of the two lovers, a supervisor monitored their intimate whispering and transmitted the lovey-dovey conversations to a second supervisor. The second supervisor recorded the passionate voice mail dialogues and played them back to Johnson's wife, Elizabeth.

The lovers' liaison ended and the marriage remained intact, but David Johnson, who was allegedly told that his voice mail would be private, confronted his employer and was promptly fired. Silver reportedly stayed with the chain and was promoted to restaurant manager.

Believing that their privacy had been violated, David and Elizabeth Johnson each sued the fast-food company for $1 million.

Mr. and Mrs. Johnson argued that voice mail messages are protected by the 1968 federal wiretap law and a 1986 amendment, the Electronic Communications

Privacy Act, and that the company's supervisor intentionally inflicted emotional anguish, embarrassment, and loss of reputation and income.

The company argued that they owned the telephone and the computer and that the monitoring was carried out for legitimate business purposes. They maintained that Johnson should have known that his boss would gain access to his voice mail and, as a result, Johnson should have had no expectation of privacy.

Nevertheless, after more than one year of legal arguments, the case was settled out of court. The terms were not disclosed, but the Johnson's lawyer reportedly stated that it had been resolved to the satisfaction of Mr. and Mrs. Johnson.

If the case had been settled in court, it might have helped determine whether conversations recorded in electronic voice mailboxes should be granted the same legal protection as hard-line telephone calls or postal mail.

At a time when voice mail has become commonplace, the right-of-privacy versus the right-to-monitor controversy is still undecided.

PROTECTING YOUR PRIVACY

♦ Companies and individual employees should face up to reality; there is a very good chance that voice mailboxes will be monitored by authorized and unauthorized eavesdroppers. Think carefully before gabbing carelessly on voice mail systems. Your messages are recorded, stored, and may be transmitted to others.

♦ Awareness is our best defense. Companies and individuals aware of the latest voice mail schemes are more likely to recognize suspicious activities and less likely to be victimized. "We were an easy mark for the tactic because we had never heard of it," admitted a Chicago-based executive.

♦ Supervisors should make sure passwords or codes are changed regularly and should deactivate the access code for any employee who resigns or is fired. Remind employees to select hard-to-break passwords. Do not use birth dates or the names of children or pets as passwords.

♦ Some new voice mail systems automatically alert users to abnormal calling patterns that could indicate fraud or mischief. These systems can be programmed to turn off whenever invalid attempts are made to access the system.

♦ Take an aggressive legal and public stand against hackers. A former employee of a large company in Andover, Massachusetts, unlawfully entered the company's voice mail system and retrieved messages from customers. Instead of handling the situation in-house, the company went public and sued the employee. This action helped the entire business community and served as a warning to other would-be hackers that espionage and sabotage would not be tolerated.

4

THEFT OF E-MAIL

Most people who use electronic mail (E-mail) believe that their messages are private. They are not. Employers are allowed by law to monitor employees' E-mail. Most people think that electronic mail messages are secured by their personal passwords. They are wrong. Treating E-mail like a fleeting form of communication, most people also believe they can just click Delete and their confidential, ill-advised, or pornographic communications will simply disappear into space. Don't count on it. The key evidence in the now-famous Iran-Contra scandal was uncovered when investigators recovered White House aide Oliver L. North's E-mail. North thought he had deleted the confidential information, but messages still remained on central computer files.

Electronic mail systems allow users to send printed electronic messages, either personal or work-related, to each other via computer. More than fifty million people in the U.S. are currently using some form of E-mail.

The Federal Electronic Communication Privacy Act of 1986 protects the confidentiality of electronic messages sent through public networks like MCI Mail or

Compuserve. The law does not apply to a company's internal electronic mail.

Treating E-mail like a sealed, stamped, personal letter, some companies warn employees not to read the electronic mail of their coworkers. The employees are told that reading another person's electronic mail is a violation of corporate ethics and may result in disciplinary action or dismissal.

Users should be advised, however, that just because something is illegal or unethical does not mean that everyone is going to obey the rule.

In 1993 a large U.S. newspaper disciplined and recalled a well-regarded foreign correspondent from its foreign bureau after he was caught reading his colleagues' electronic mail.

Other correspondents in the bureau became suspicious when they discovered that their passwords had been entered into the computer system at times when they were not present. Fortunately, the newspaper's computer system was designed to keep a record of each time an employee used his password to log onto the system.

Setting up a sting operation, someone at another of the newspaper's foreign bureaus sent two electronic mail messages with false, eye-opening information to a journalist in the first bureau. Taking the bait, the targeted journalist intercepted the messages, which were not directed to his mailbox, and verbally inquired about their content.

Many E-mail users wrongly assume that the recipient of their messages will be discreet and will not forward the mail to other readers. Air Force Capt. Scott Zobrist learned the hard way that it can be very dangerous to assume.

After the now-famous rescue of Air Force pilot Scott O'Grady in Bosnia, Capt. Zobrist, who was stationed with Capt. O'Grady in Italy, sent an E-mail message to a few close military friends.

"Pray for the U.N. leadership to get a clue and let us blow these bastards back into the Stone Age," Capt. Zobrist wrote of the Bosnian Serbs.

Much to the Pentagon's chagrin, Capt. Zobrist's message was passed from computer to computer until finally it was publicly available on the Internet.

Researchers of aggressive driving have recorded large numbers of normally polite and rational individuals who become tyrannical maniacs when they get behind the wheel. Many people behave in a similar manner when they get behind a computer.

Feeling anonymous, many E-mail users drive recklessly down the information superhighway, carelessly hurling epithets and insults like empty beer cans. Sometimes called *flaming* in computer jargon, this type of behavior can be deadly to careers and personal lives.

A Los Angeles police officer learned this lesson after the highly criticized Rodney King beating in 1991. Mistakenly believing that his E-mail message would be funny and private, the officer typed a message into his squad car computer that made all police officers look bad: "Oops!—I haven't beaten anyone this bad in a long time." The officer's insensitive message appeared in newspapers nationwide.

Encased in his metal womb, the aggressive driver feels safe blasting his horn, flashing his high beams, and hurling obscene gestures. He or she is usually oblivious to the fact that 1,500 people are killed or injured each year as a result of silly traffic disputes.

Hiding behind the Delete key, the aggressive E-mail user feels perfectly safe spewing sexual slurs and attacking the integrity of bosses and coworkers. As with the aggressive motorist, the aggressive E-mail user is not as safe as he thinks.

Most E-mail users don't realize that they don't have absolute control over where their messages go and that a high percentage of deleted E-mail messages are actually saved and stored in the computer system. In fact, most computer systems are engineered to save data, not delete it.

An employee we will call Mud who had been with a Maryland-based communications firm for thirteen years, vented his rage and sent a scathing message concerning the CEO to his confidant in another office. Logging on the next morning, the horrified confidant read the incredibly offensive message and immediately pushed Delete. She then phoned the sender and warned him to delete the original, which he did.

There was only one small problem. The two employees were not aware that the system's supervisor always made backup tapes of everything on the computer and then stored those tapes for years.

"My name is Mud," said the employee when the CEO was informed of the crude and insulting message. "How could I have been so stupid?" After eleven months of job hunting, it is assumed that Mud is now wiser and less reckless.

In another case, a New Jersey man sued his wife for

divorce, claiming adultery, after he retrieved her steamy E-mail messages. Thinking that her messages were secret, the man's wife had carried on a torrid extramarital relationship via E-mail.

Employees frequently download electronic mail onto their desktop PC, storing the messages on the hard drive. When this occurs, a push of the Delete key doesn't erase the messages, it merely makes that section on the hard drive available for new data. The messages that were supposedly erased can still be retrieved and read.

E-mail messages often fall into unintended hands through carelessness and poor security. Dozens of sensitive E-mails have been discovered when recipients left them on office copiers. In some cases, supervisors have taken the liberty of copying office computer files.

Electronic mail has revolutionized communication in the workplace and is here to stay. Users would be well advised to be more businesslike with their business communication and to realize that E-mail is a long way from being private.

PROTECTING YOUR PRIVACY

♦ Don't put anything on E-mail that you wouldn't want a boss, a jury, or an unauthorized outsider to see. Think carefully about what you say and to whom you say it.

♦ Understand that clicking the Delete button does not necessarily mean your E-mail message is completely erased. New technological advances are continually adding more automatic backups, more storage capacity, and more redundancies to prevent accidental erasure. Deleted messages often survive because someone downloads an E-mail message onto a hard drive or makes a backup tape. Computer systems are increasingly being designed to save data, not delete it.

♦ It is a mistake to compare E-mail to a legally protected, stamped, and sealed envelope. Electronic mail is more like a postcard that gets passed from hand to hand.

♦ Remember that when someone sues a company or an individual, the rules of discovery demand that all relevant records, including E-mail messages, be provided to the court. Lawyers have long recognized that E-mail can provide a gold mine of unguarded information about the company or the individual they are suing. There are experts who specialize in retrieving E-mail messages that were thought to have been erased.

♦ Don't be an E-mail drunk. Give a person a few too many drinks and he or she may communicate in a rude, unguarded, and uninhibited

manner. E-mail systems have the same intoxi-
cating effect on some people. Sober up!

♦ Don't be naive. Just because the law protects
the confidentiality of messages sent through
public networks does not mean the law will always be obeyed. In reality, most people who illegally steal E-mail are never discovered,
caught, or prosecuted.

♦ As a safeguard, utilize E-mail systems that record
who has logged on to send or retrieve a message
and the time the communication occurred.

♦ Users would be well advised to protect their
passwords as they would their house keys. Give
a person the key to your E-mail, and they can
steal whatever they want, night or day. Be aware
that would-be burglars often use ploys to obtain passwords and that some intruders will
come in through the back door or devise a way
to bypass security.

♦ If an E-mail message is to be protected, shred or
pulverize printouts before discarding them. Do
not leave hard copies on unoccupied desks, on
duplicating machines, or in unlocked cabinets.

♦ Remember, just because you practice good security does not mean the recipient of your
message does the same. Security is only as
strong as its weakest link.

5

OBSCENE AND HARASSING PHONE CALLS

Carrie, a twenty-nine-year-old single mother and substitute teacher, received the vulgar, late-night calls two or three times a week for four months. "His theme was always the same," Carrie told the police. Using graphic and degrading language, "he would blurt out disgusting things he wanted to do to me sexually."

At first, Carrie dismissed the caller as "some jerk looking for a cheap thrill." But then the caller began focusing his attention on Carrie's six-year-old daughter.

"He mentioned her by name and told me horrible things he was going to do to her," Carrie explained. It was nineteen months since Carrie had received a call, but the look in her eyes and her clenched fists revealed that she was still frightened and still angry. "I'm not kidding; I'd cut his balls off and blow his brains out if I caught him," said the normally demure elementary schoolteacher. "It was so scary because sometimes he would know what clothes my daughter had been wearing earlier in the day."

Taping the "bastard's" conversation on three occasions, Carrie played the tapes for coworkers, neighbors, and people at her health club in hopes that someone would recognize his voice. "I'm convinced that the caller was someone from work or the health club," Carrie insisted. "I think he got word that I was passing around the tapes and got scared." Carrie is just one of more than one hundred thousand women, men, and children who receive obscene or harassing phone calls every day in the United States. As the following three cases will illustrate, obscene calls are a cruel invasion of privacy and are often perpetrated by so-called pillars of society.

THE BANKER

On May 19, 1992, Mitchell Beck, forty-seven, a former vice president of operations at American Mortgage Investment Corp. in Philadelphia, was sentenced to three and a half to ten years in prison for making more than one hundred obscene and threatening calls to women.

Telephoning women at random, Beck would convincingly tell them that he had kidnapped their husbands or boyfriends. The hostage would be released, Beck would say, only if the women complied with his demands. In most cases, Beck coerced the women to undress, describe sexual experiences, or masturbate (sometimes in front of windows). While some women promptly hung up, others, including some children, followed his orders out of fear for their loved ones.

Typically, the calls were made from Beck's office between 7 A.M. and 9 A.M. He seemed to know when the women's husbands or boyfriends left for work.

Beck ordered a woman in Bucks County, Pennsylvania, to go into her garage with her eleven-year-old son, disrobe, and have her son fondle her. Scared to tears for her husband, the woman complied.

Many of the victims were convinced that the caller actually held their husbands or boyfriends captive because he knew their names and other details of their lives. It's possible that Beck gained access to some of the information at work.

Police stormed Beck's office after a woman who had received a threatening call utilized a caller identification feature on her telephone and traced the call to the American Mortgage Investment Corp.

Investigators soon learned that Beck, a married man with three sons, had been incarcerated fifteen years earlier for making 248 similar calls.

Haunted by their ordeal, many of Beck's victims sought psychiatric counseling and suffered problems such as depression, sleeplessness, and post-traumatic stress disorder.

THE COLLEGE PRESIDENT

Richard Berendzen, the MIT- and Harvard-educated president of American University, in Washington, D.C., had a penchant for making obscene telephone calls. Closing the door to his private office on the campus of

American University, Berendzen made repeated calls to female child-care providers in which he would describe, in detail, his fantasies of having sexual relations with children.

On April 8, 1990, shortly after police traced the bizarre calls to his office, Berendzen, who usually worked over one hundred hours a week, resigned from the A.U. presidency. He later pleaded guilty to making obscene telephone calls and was sentenced to two thirty-day jail terms that were suspended on the condition that he continue psychiatric counseling.

To his credit, Berendzen took responsibility for his behavior, wrote a book about the childhood incest he suffered at the hands of his parents, and continues to seek counseling. His book, *Come Here: A Man Overcomes the Tragic Aftermath of Childhood Sexual Abuse*, chronicles the sexual abuse inflicted upon him more than forty years earlier by his mentally ill mother.

THE U.S. CUSTOMS AGENT

Susan Billig's ordeal started on March 5, 1974, when her beautiful, raven-haired, seventeen-year-old daughter, Amy, an accomplished flutist, disappeared while hitchhiking. For the next twenty-one years, a faceless monster entered her home late at night via the telephone and forced her to listen to his sex talk with teases that he knew Amy's whereabouts.

"At first I hung up on him, but then I thought he might know something about Amy," Billig would later tell the court. Since there was a chance the caller actually had knowledge of Amy's whereabouts, Billig didn't dare change her phone number.

The calls began three weeks after the police and the media announced Amy's disappearance. In a gruff, menacing voice, a man who said his name was Hal Johnson falsely confessed to Susan Billig that he had kidnapped Amy, sexually abused her, and sold her as a sex slave to a motorcycle gang.

The heartbroken mother would plead with Johnson to tell her more about Amy. "Are you sure she's well?" Mrs. Billig knew she was dealing with a sick man, but there was always the possibility that he really did know something about Amy.

Relentlessly toying with Mrs. Billig, Johnson would sometimes call seven times a day with taunts, threats, and mockery; sometimes the phone wouldn't ring for weeks. But the calls always resumed, and Mrs. Billing was forced to listen to sadistic sex talk in exchange for false clues. "Amy's body is magnificent," Johnson told Mrs. Billig.

"He wanted me to be part of a mother-daughter sex team, asked if I had two breasts, all kinds of sexual things I can't mention," Billig, then seventy, told the court.

Johnson frustrated the police and the FBI for twenty-one years by using pay phones. Authorities would trace every call, but Johnson would have left when they arrived. In 1993, Johnson began using an "untraceable" cellular phone.

Using the latest technology, police on October 27, 1995, traced the cellular calls and the phone records to

Henry Johnson Blair, a forty-six-year-old supervisor with the U.S. Customs Service in Miami.

Investigators would soon learn that Blair's calls to Billig were part of a larger, more bizarre pattern in which he called several vulnerable mothers of murdered, missing, or troubled women.

On March 29, 1996, Henry Johnson Blair, forty-eight, stood before the court in handcuffs and leg irons. As his wife and two grown daughters looked on, the judge denounced him as a coward and sentenced him to two years in jail.

"He harassed that poor woman for twenty-one years," complained a policewoman close to the case. "That monster invaded her serenity. . . . He deserves much more than two years!"

There is no one profile of an obscene phone caller, but the offending behaviors are often triggered by stress and suppressed anger. Many offenders were sexually abused as children.

Men who make obscene phone calls usually lead outwardly normal lives but have serious doubts about their gender identity. They make obscene calls to feel powerful and to reassure themselves of their masculinity. Serving as an antidote to anxiety, most calls are made when the men are under extreme stress. Misdirecting their rage, the obscene phone caller reduces tension and gets turned on by hurting others.

Many offenders will use a ruse to lure unwitting victims into phone sex. In Maryland, a man who claimed to be affiliated with a local hospital pretended to be conducting a medical survey concerning circumcision. At first, his questions were nonthreatening. "Does your religion disallow circumcision?" the caller asked one woman. "But then he asked if I enjoyed looking at my son's erection."

In New Jersey, a responsible-sounding caller posing as a Macy's department store representative told women they had won a shopping spree, then tried to talk them into getting undressed. Telling the women they had won ten complete outfits, the man then asked about their dress sizes. When the women communicated that they felt uncomfortable discussing their clothing sizes with a stranger, the caller replied in a reassuring, businesslike tone, "Oh, dear, don't worry—I do this all the time."

After asking about their dress sizes, the man explained that the shopping spree included free underwear. "We'll need to know your bra and panty sizes," the man requested nonchalantly. If the women didn't hesitate to give their underwear sizes, the man would ask them to get undressed, supposedly to discern how many outfits they could put on in a set period of time. Once the women were naked, he would ask them to touch themselves. Fooled into phone sex, some angry victims explained that they felt emotionally raped.

Entering homes and offices uninvited, the obscene phone caller is a faceless monster who murders serenity, commits emotional rape, and destroys our sense of privacy.

PROTECTING YOUR PRIVACY

♦ Hang up at the first obscene word. If the caller doesn't say anything, hang up after you've said hello for the second time.

♦ Never give out any information to the caller such as your name, your children's names, your address, place of employment, or whether you are home alone.

♦ Instruct your children not to give any information out to strangers. Tell them not to be fooled by someone they don't recognize who calls them by name or claims to be a relative.

♦ If you receive persistent or repeated harassing or obscene calls, report the problem to your telephone service representative. This number is usually listed in the front of your telephone book. The telephone company may offer to put a trap on your line, which will trace all calls made to your number.

♦ Consider getting a second phone in your home under a different number. One woman listened to her harasser on one phone while a family member called the police on a second phone. This gave police enough time to trace the call and arrest the perpetrator before he could flee.

♦ Consider changing to an unlisted number.

♦ Notify police immediately if you receive a threatening telephone call. All threats are to be taken seriously.

♦ Be careful where you display your phone number. I know of nineteen cases in which obscene callers have copied phone numbers from women's exercise cards at health clubs. Some weirdos have obtained numbers from the For Sale signs women have placed in their car windows. In other known cases, they overheard their targets giving out phone numbers to receptionists, merchants, and others.

♦ Try to get a tape recording of the harasser's voice and monologue. The tape will help identify the caller and will help the police and the prosecutors put him in jail. Always save obscene messages left on your answering machine.

♦ Keep a log of all harassing calls, recording the time, date, and duration of the call, language the caller used and, if you have Caller ID, the number from which he or she called. This information will be vital in catching and prosecuting the caller.

♦ Don't fall for ruses that trick you into participating in phone sex. Be leery of surveys that require you to answer intimate medical questions and phony department store representatives who inquire about your undergarments, shoes, or dress size.

♦ New technologies, such as Caller ID and Call Tracing, Call Block, and Anonymous Call Rejection, which allow you to identify the caller before picking up and to trace the phone your caller is using, are excellent security tools. Services vary from town to town, so ask your telephone representative to explain all the security options. Be aware, however, that the harasser can block the service by dialing certain codes such as *57 before dialing your number. This code will prevent his phone number from appearing on your display device. These new technologies have resulted in the capture of dozens of obscene callers.

6

GUARDING YOUR GARBAGE

The first step for the five gang members was to recover the computerized payroll printouts, discarded by the Philadelphia School District, from a paper recycling center. The printouts contained detailed financial and biographical information, including names, titles, addresses, and Social Security numbers of teachers, secretaries, administrators, and other school district employees—the information they would need to turn trash into cash.

Using the names and information taken from the trash, the gang members made phony driver's licences and other identification. Like magic—abracadabra— the thieves turned themselves into teachers.

Armed with the fake identification, the gang opened phony bank accounts with small cash deposits. When the checks and ATM cards arrived, the gang made large deposits with bad checks. Exploiting a banking policy that makes deposits available within twenty-four hours, even before the checks clear, the fraud ring had a limited amount of time to withdraw the money before the bank caught on.

Soon after the checks and ATM cards arrived in the

mail, the criminals received applications for credit cards from major financial institutions. Naturally, the gang used the teachers' names and Social Security numbers to apply for the credit cards. When the credit cards arrived, the shopping spree began. "Who says teachers don't make a lot of money," the crooks must have joked. They stole nearly $500,000 from banks and stores, recycling garbage into gold.

One hundred innocent school district employees with good credit and good reputations were eventually labeled deadbeats and would receive strongly worded dunning notices for debts they had not incurred. Bill collectors showed up on their doorsteps and their credit ratings took years to repair.

A computer hacker enters your computer and steals valuable information. A Dumpster diver enters your trash and steals the same information. Garbage in, gold out.

A bag of trash speaks eloquently of your sexual, social, and shopping habits. Letters discarded in 1995 by well-known individuals in three states alerted gossip mongers that a socialite was on the verge of bankruptcy, that a rabbi's daughter had undergone an abortion, and that a CEO's son had confessed to being gay. "Dad, I'm not ashamed of being gay, but I think it would hurt all of us if I came out of the closet, so to speak, and went public . . ." the letter stated. Unfortunately, the decision was taken out of their hands when they discarded the letter.

Discarded prescription bottles can tell a stalker, a nosy neighbor, or a political rival that you are taking an antianxiety drug and the label might indicate that you are seeing a psychiatrist or that your child is taking Ritalin for attention deficit disorder. In Washington, D.C., an anonymous stalker found an empty antiviral medication tube in a woman's trash. "I see you have herpes," the mysterious caller told the frightened twenty-nine-year-old woman at 3 A.M.

Articles found in your trash speak volumes—right or wrong—about your sex life. A curious sixty-eight-year-old grandmother was shocked to see that her new neighbor's fifteen-year-old daughter was taking birth control pills. When the new neighbor learned that this accurate information was circulated around the neighborhood, the grandmother was forced to admit that she often picked through people's trash.

A private investigator, hired by a divorce attorney, found six condom wrappers in a woman's trash while looking for evidence of an affair. Other items the investigator found in the Monday-morning pickup included seventeen assorted bourbon, scotch, and vodka miniatures (she was dating an airline pilot), two empty containers of blond hair dye, used round-trip tickets to New York and Chicago (the pilot's route), and the smoking gun, i.e., a faxed, X-rated message from the alleged lover. As it turned out, the woman's estranged husband was not the only person who found the contents of her trash interesting. The pilot's wife was enlightened as well.

"It's usually women who hire me to check up on their boyfriends," explained the investigator, who jokingly referred to himself as an expert in "garbagology." He typically looked for matchbooks from disreputable places, credit card receipts for local hotel rooms, and phone bills with suspicious numbers. "If you really want the dirt on someone, you go through their trash."

"If you are what you throw away," said a man in sub-urban Maryland, "then my next-door neighbor is a phony and a hypocrite." The writer "couldn't help but notice" that his neighbor, an outspoken environmen-talist, was not recycling his paper, plastic, or metal cans. "However, he does rent an awful lot of triple X-rated adult movies, and either he or his wife wears Depend undergarments."

A diver's favorite find is a preapproved credit card application. "I made over $230,000 in one year with those babies and blew it all on crack," said a former New York accountant who is currently in a court-ordered rehabilitation program. "It's easier than rob-bing a bank, and you get a lot more money."

After filling out the change of address on the preap-proved credit card application, the diver mails the ap-plication to the bank and waits for the card to arrive. He or she can then charge merchandise under the name of the person to whom the application was origi-nally sent.

"No wonder the credit card companies are losing over $3 billion a year," said the crack-addicted accoun-tant. "The banks don't give a shit because they just pass the losses on to the consumer."

Whether you think "garbagology" is a good or bad thing probably depends on the situation. If someone finds embarrassing or damaging material in your trash, you would probably consider it an invasion of privacy. But if a murderer, rapist, spy, or white-collar crook is convicted because of what the police find in his trash, you would probably think it's great.

Hundreds of drug traffickers have been identified because police discovered razor blades, straws containing cocaine residue, syringes, and other drug-related paraphernalia in their garbage. The discarded phone records of the addict and the trafficker often identify other addicts and other drug traffickers. "And when that happens, we search their trash, too," said a federal officer stationed in Washington, D.C.

Just as anthropologists reconstruct ancient civilizations from the debris left behind, Dumpster divers can surveil your everyday life, reconstruct your personal and financial history—and invade your privacy.

LIFTING THE LID ON GARBAGE
—— *A Chronicle of Important Incidents* ——

1975—Washington, D.C.: Reporters with the *National Enquirer* made off with five bags of trash from the home of Secretary of State Henry Kissinger. Secretary Kissinger was reportedly embarrassed when the newspaper published its gleanings.

1979—Iran: When radical, armed students seized the U.S. embassy in Iran, security officers, U.S. Marine guards, and other embassy personnel were ordered to shred all important documents. Recovering the shredded documents, the students patiently pieced them back together. It turned out to be an intelligence gold mine for the new Iranian government.

1991—Florida: Dubbed the Jailhouse Shopping Network by the media, investigators discovered that inmates, using prison telephones, had illegally charged $6 million worth of merchandise using other people's credit cards. Friends on the outside were supplying the inmates with credit card slips obtained from hotel Dumpsters.

1993—Oregon: Someone stole ten bags of trash from the home of Elaine Franklin, Senator Bob Packwood's chief of staff. The garbage heist may have been an effort to obtain information about her boss. Senator Packwood was the target of a Senate Ethics Committee investigation into allegations that he made unwanted sexual advances to 23 women. "It was an infringement of my privacy," said Franklin.

1993—Virginia: A torn yellow adhesive note recovered from a trash can outside the home of then-CIA officer Aldrich H. Ames gave the FBI its first usable piece of evidence that the veteran counter-intelligence expert was the Russian spy they had been seeking for nine years. In a high-risk trash cover, two members of the FBI's special surveillance group (SSG) took Ames's curbside trash can and exchanged it with a similar container. The torn note recovered from the trash was a penciled draft of one that Ames attached to secret documents he had given the Russians a week earlier.

1995—Georgia: Federal authorities smashed a sophisticated fraud ring and arrested thirty people who stole more than $10 million in dozens of states by recovering discarded checks, deposit slips, and credit card receipts from Dumpsters and trash bins. Using information gleaned from Dumpsters, the gang used high-quality computer graphics to make fake driver's licenses and Social Security cards, which were then used to create phony checking accounts, to cash counterfeit checks, make unauthorized credit card purchases, and even file false tax returns.

1996—New Jersey: East Hanover detectives arrested two Dumpster divers who rifled the trash of New Jersey banks to obtain old account numbers and names that they used to write and cash phony checks. The criminals knew that an account may be closed at one bank branch, but it sometimes takes several days for that information to reach other branches. Using the information obtained from the trash, the criminals were cashing phony checks all over New Jersey. The case revealed a careless yet widespread practice among banks who dumped old checks, account numbers, and customer financial information in unsecured Dumpsters.

1997—Pennsylvania: A multimillion-dollar credit card scheme run by inmates, much like the Jailhouse Shopping Network in Florida, was uncovered at Graterford Prison. Using prison telephones, the inmates ordered more than $2 million in computers, televisions, jewelry, and other items utilizing credit card numbers stolen from hotel Dumpsters nationwide. Friends and relatives on the outside would raid the hotel Dumpsters and provide the numbers to the inmates. Hundreds of innocent credit card owners had their privacy invaded and their credit destroyed by crooks who were already incarcerated.

PROTECTING YOUR PRIVACY

♦ Papers containing any kind of financial or personal information should be torn up in tiny pieces, shredded, or burned. If you are throwing away lots of sensitive information at once, dispose of half in one trash bag, half in another, and set them outside on separate days. Take your trash outside as close to collection time as possible. Be especially careful to destroy preapproved credit card applications and documents that contain your Social Security number or credit card information.

♦ Don't assume that someone going through your trash is just a homeless person. Many

Dumpster divers disguise themselves as homeless people and many ringleaders hire drug addicts and alcoholics to collect items from the
trash. Believe it or not, the Dumpster-diving
underground has become so lucrative that
many gangs use strong-arm tactics to keep
other divers away from their turf.

♦ Not all trash is stolen from curbside receptacles
or back lot Dumpsters. Many ringleaders hire
dishonest janitors, clerks, secretaries, and other
employees to collect the trash from inside
rental agencies, hotels, hospitals, and so forth.
In other words, your sensitive business trash
may never make it to a Dumpster.

♦ If your business information is particularly sensitive, consider hiring a firm that specializes in
pulverizing documents, a method that dices
and slices to make sure that no one can reconstruct your discarded papers. In the past, determined snoopers have pieced shredded
secrets back together. McDonald's Corporation, the Pittsburgh Pirates, and even the FBI
pay to have their sensitive documents pulver-
ized.

♦ Sensitive business information should be
shredded before being transported to a recycling center, incinerator, or pulverizing firm.
Many divers (often hired by rivals) will bribe

truck drivers or simply obtain the documents when they arrive at the final destination.

♦ Judging from hundreds of financial horror stories, divers focus most of their attention on Dumpsters at banks, hotels, travel agencies, restaurants, service stations, pharmacies, hospitals, and airline ticket offices. Nevertheless, divers still target hundreds of thousands of individual home owners each year.

♦ Before discarding something, ask yourself, "How could a stalker, a gossip, a criminal, or a competitor use this information?" A legal document concerning a divorce might divulge extremely private information about your finances, children, and sexual relationship. A stalker in Massachusetts knew where his victim exercised because he obtained a health club membership receipt from her trash. A prescription container or an insurance document might disclose medical information you consider private. Your long-distance phone bills and credit card bills are considered a gold mine for a wide range of marketing specialists and other snoops. Huge amounts of information can be learned simply by reviewing your grocery store receipts.

♦ Modernizing information storage systems, more and more companies are inputting thousands of medical, financial, and private personnel files into computers and are discarding mountains of documents once stored on paper. Dozens of highly publicized privacy horror stories resulted from improper disposal of these documents. Companies, schools, and hospitals have an obligation to insure that private and public information does not fall into the wrong hands.

7

LISTENING DEVICES

Twenty-five-year-old Dennis Roy Layton of South Carolina, didn't want his fourteen-year-old girlfriend to tell anyone—especially her parents—that they were having a sexual relationship.

Telling the girl that he was psychic and that his powers were granted to him by God, he sternly warned her that he could read her mind and he would know if she shared their sexual secrets with anyone.

In truth, Layton did seem to be psychic; he had an uncanny knowledge of the girl's conversations, her parents' conversations, and their plans and schedules. If the girl had a private talk with her best friend, Layton would be able to repeat the entire conversation the next day. The girl would join her family in an impromptu get-together across town, and like magic, Layton would show up. His paranormal powers must have been both amazing and frightening to the naive fourteen-year-old girl.

But Layton was not psychic. He was an eavesdropper. Layton installed a listening device in a clock radio and gave the radio to his girlfriend as a gift. Refusing to fall for the "powers from God" explanation, the girl's parents searched her room and, as one investigator said, "started putting two and two together."

On March 7, 1995, Layton was convicted of violating federal eavesdropping laws and was told he also faced rape charges in state court for having sex with a minor.

Technological advances, in recent years, have spawned spying devices that put Maxwell Smart's shoe-phone to shame. Today, you can buy miniature listening devices that fit into ballpoint pens, Rolex watches, silver dollars, beer cans, or a package of cigarettes.

Anyone who wants to eavesdrop on a lover or a neighbor or steal clients and trade secrets from a business competitor can purchase a $30 to $40 transmitter/microphone, smaller than a cigarette lighter and conceal the device in a potted plant.

A construction company owner supplied three of his female employees and a client with brand-new handheld calculators. Each calculator concealed a built-in transmitter that allowed the man to spy on their conversations from a distance of 600 yards. "I don't know if the jerk is paranoid, kinky, or both," ranted a twenty-six-year-old secretary when she discovered that her privacy had been violated. "This is worse than being sexually harassed."

Listening devices take many different forms. Security experts have long been aware of a telephone that lets a caller listen to everyone in the room. The phone has a built-in room monitor and looks and works like any standard telephone. The eavesdropper, who can be thousands of miles away, simply dials a number and is able to hear all room and telephone conversations, even if the phone is on the cradle and out of use. Since the phone doesn't ring, nobody in the room is suspicious. "I bought mine in California, but I saw the same model for sale in Chicago," said a Maryland real estate developer who unabashedly admitted, "I've got one in my guest room at home and one at the beach house." I was uncomfortable when I remembered that he once offered his beach house to me for a week.

Many eavesdroppers have utilized the automatic answering feature on cellular phones to secretly invade people's privacy. The eavesdropper can leave the cellular phone in an area he wants to monitor, turn off the ringer, and call the phone from another location. The cellular phone answers automatically but doesn't ring, so the outside caller is able to hear everything that is being said.

Bugged briefcases have become very popular with industrial espionage agents, with employers who want to spy on their employees, and with employees who want to spy on their employers. They are also popular with businesspeople trying to close a deal.

Although they look like any other businessman's briefcase, there are thousands of briefcases in circulation that house secret taping and transmitting devices. In some cases, the listening device is activated simply by moving a pen from one compartment to another or by flipping a switch concealed beneath the handle.

"We were in the conference room trying to negotiate a contract with a bunch of hospital administrators," explained Kevin, a successful medical services salesman. "My partner has one of those bugged briefcases, so we left it behind when he and I went to lunch. He pulled an earpiece from his pocket and there we were eating tuna sandwiches and listening to everything the administrators were saying about us in the conference room . . . you know, what their objections were, how much our competitors were charging, and stuff like that. We went back after lunch with answers to their objections and quoted them a price slightly less than the other guys were offering. Ain't modern technology wonderful!"

Privacy invaders are also very fond of bugged ball-point pens.

"You know how sometimes you loan someone a pen to sign something and they inadvertently put the pen in their own pocket?" the spy store salesman asked rhetorically. "Well with this pen you might *want* that to happen." He laughed. "Whenever someone is near this pen, you'll be able to monitor what is being said."

Concealing tiny but powerful transmitters, these expensive-looking pens rarely arouse suspicion "because you can actually write with them and everybody carries a pen."

"You could just slip the pen into your girlfriend's purse or leave it on a competitor's desk," the salesman slyly suggested. "Even if they discover that it's bugged, they won't know who is listening."

An insidious invasion of privacy, the business of surreptitious surveillance poses a serious threat to civil liberty, personhood, and the public's right to tell the world to mind its own business. We need to increase our awareness of the threat, aggressively pursue the perpetrators, and loudly communicate that illegal snooping is a reprehensible act that we will not tolerate.

THE SPY STORES

John Demeter, the owner of Spy Shops International, a chain of stores that illegally sold electronic listening devices to James Bond aficionados, and anyone else who wanted to eavesdrop on private conversations, was sentenced to three years in federal prison on January 15, 1997.

The crackdown began in 1994 when authorities raided forty so-called spy stores in twenty-four cities including New York, Chicago, Philadelphia, San Francisco, Atlanta, Dallas, and Miami. The raids led to charges against ten Americans and three Japanese.

Under the 1968 Omnibus Crime and Safe Streets Act, it is illegal for ordinary citizens to own, manufacture, or sell eavesdropping equipment specifically designed for "the surreptitious interception of wire, oral, or electric communication." But the laws did not stop stores from selling these items and did not stop aspiring secret agents from buying them.

The spy stores had tens of thousands of customers, drawn to cleverly concealed miniaturized electronic surveillance interception devices in such items as calculators, pens, briefcases, lightbulbs, desk clocks, and electric wall outlets. It is assumed that a high percentage of these customers used the listening devices for illegal purposes.

Federal agents discovered one of the store's listening devices when they intercepted a smuggled container of cocaine. The device allowed drug traffickers to tell if the shipment had been discovered. Known in the trade as a bug, another device was used by a limo driver who was hoping to get some good information on some of his celebrity clients. Another bug was used to steal trade secrets in an industrial espionage case.

Most of the stores posted signs firmly directing purchasers not to misuse the products pretending to safeguard privacy. One such store sold phone-tapping equipment to an undercover agent posing as a Russian national, who refused to show any identification. The salesperson instructed the customer on how to tap a U.S. phone.

It is also naive to think that warning labels on eavesdropping equipment will prevent customers from using the device for eavesdropping.

Many spy stores sold the Bionic Ear, a sophisticated, handheld, long-distance microphone that can pick up a whisper at one hundred yards. "You could point this at two lovers on a park bench and hear every word they say," a salesman told me. "A lawyer client of mine bought one of these to listen to other lawyers," he said proudly. Incredibly, the disclaimer label on the Bionic Ear read: "Not to be used for eavesdropping."

Suppose you need to break into a home or office to plant an electric wall outlet bug or to install a secret video camera or to hide in someone's closet? Not to worry. The spy stores also sell books on how to pick locks. "We can't sell you the actual lock picks unless you are a locksmith," the attendant explained rather self-righteously. "But I can give you an address in Texas where you can order them."

"Why would an ordinary citizen want a set of lock picks?" I inquired. "Well, suppose you get locked out of your home," he responded with a wink and a nod.

Pleading ignorance, the defendants in the nation-wide spy store sting argued that they didn't know it was illegal to sell listening devices in the United States. If that's true, then why did they try to disguise the company and the imported products? Investigators discovered that the owners set up a shell company—Put God First International—and mislabeled privacy-invasion devices so they could be imported from Japan.

Cracking down on the customers of the multimillion-dollar spy industry, police have arrested businessmen, con artists, and many other professionals who purchased the illegal equipment.

"We plan more arrests in the future," explained a task force member. "But thousands of people who bought illegal spy devices will probably get away with using them."

The chairman of a large company in Kentucky was accused of buying a powerful listening device to spy on a female employee. The employee reportedly had access to information that the chairman was worried about.

"I know of seventeen high-level business executives who bought bugs to spy on employees, mistresses, and competitors," said a police official who asked not to be identified.

In 1995, authorities charged the president of a northeast company with purchasing $14,000 worth of bugging equipment. "His company makes plastics," explained a New York attorney who was not involved in the case. "Why would he purchase $14,000 worth of bugging equipment disguised as pens, calculators, and electric wall plugs?"

The listening devices sold by spy stores nationwide range in price from $30 to thousands of dollars. But if a customer uses one of these spy gadgets for illegal purposes, the price could be considerably steeper. It is a federal crime, punishable by up to five years in prison and a $250,000 fine, to intercept oral communications without the consent of the parties.

HOW WIDESPREAD IS THE PROBLEM?

Thousands of illegal listening devices are known to have been concealed in private homes and apartments, businesses, schools, hotel rooms, and government installations. Illegal bugs have also been placed in limousines, taxis, aircraft, yachts, and ships. These devices have been used by a wide range of industrial espionage agents, jealous spouses and stalkers, private investigators, sex offenders, journalists, and nosy neighbors and landlords. The following are examples of this unconscionable invasion of privacy.

August 20, 1992—Richmond, Virginia: Gubernatorial chief of staff J. T. Shropshire discovered a match box-sized transmitter in his office after it fell from beneath his desk during a meeting with a state legislator.

October 25, 1993—Chicago, Illinois: Millionaire businessman Robert J. Tezak pleaded guilty to burning down a bowling alley for the insurance money and to threatening to kill his former daughter-in-law and her family if she became a witness against him. Tezak learned that his daughter-in-law had planned to testify against him by bugging her Phoenix hotel room in December 1992.

December 3, 1993—Nacogdoches, Texas: Officials of Stephen F. Austin State University discovered several electronic listening devices in the third-floor offices of the school administration building, including those of the university president and three vice presidents.

July 27, 1994—Detroit, Michigan: Mario Weber, twenty-eight, was sentenced to ten to fifteen years for sexually abusing a ten-year-old boy. While pursuing the child, Weber used sophisticated technology to bug the boy's home and eavesdrop on the family's telephone conversations. By monitoring the family's activities, Weber was able to arrange meetings with the child and determine if he was talking about their relationship.

March 17, 1995—Charleston, West Virginia: A state Senator was charged with paying two men to wiretap the telephone of his former wife, a high-ranking official. The couple had been involved in a custody dispute over their daughter.

June 14, 1995—Miami, Florida: Four American business executives flying out of Miami reportedly discovered two sophisticated listening devices in their corporate aircraft. One bug was concealed beneath a seat, and the other was hidden in an undisclosed location.

November 5, 1995—Florida: A political candidate for the city council and a local businessman were charged with plotting to tap a phone in the city manager's office, hoping to gather dirt on city leaders. They were also accused of trying to hire a prostitute to seduce the mayor.

June 24, 1996—Tallahassee, Florida: Peter R. Rayner, a private investigator, pleaded guilty to bugging a state insurance official's home telephone. Bankers Insurance Co. admitted hiring the private investigator to dig up dirt on Kevin McCarty, an assistant division chief in the Department of Insurance, but denied ordering the illegal wiretap. Insurance Commissioner Bill Nelson stated that he was outraged that a company would hire a private investigator to spy on a state official.

October 2, 1996—New York, New York: Photographer Carlos Arriazu Sanchez and Carlos Fernandez, a Miami-based private detective, were sentenced to six months in jail for eavesdropping on Giselle Howard, a twenty-six-year-old former model. The two men tapped Howard's phone because she had been romantically involved with Prince Felipe, the future King of Spain, and they were hoping to sell her most intimate secrets to a celebrity magazine. The eavesdroppers gained access to the basement of Howard's apartment building and wired a high-frequency transmitter to her telephone line.

January 6, 1997—Chicago, Illinois: A wealthy socialite discovered a voice-activated listening and taping device hooked up to her apartment telephone. After sixteen years of marriage, the woman was separated from her husband and was in the process of a bitter divorce. As with all such cases, the listening device violated the rights of the woman and all of the people she spoke to on the telephone.

PROTECTING YOUR PRIVACY

♦ Prevention is the best defense. A high percentage of all cases involving illegal listening devices could have been prevented if there had been better physical security. Good security includes proper access controls, locked doors and windows, better control of keys, and the presence of well-trained security guards during and after regular working hours. One spy for hire bugged an executive's office after the cleaning staff left every door in the building unlocked. Another eavesdropper had no problem stealing the office manager's keys.

♦ Have a privacy-protection expert periodically sweep your phones, offices, and conference rooms for hidden listening devices. Relying on experience, physical inspection, and the latest technology, a specialist is far more likely to discover concealed devices than an enthusiastic but untrained security guard. Finding taps is tedious and time-consuming work. A true expert will unscrew electrical wall outlets, open telephone handsets, lift ceiling panels, and spend a lot of time on his hands and knees. One company that specializes in electronic countermeasures reportedly discovered listening devices in 85 of the 500 corporate sites they inspected.

♦ Consult with an electronic countermeasures security specialist for information on the latest antibugging technology appropriate for your situation.

♦ Train your employees and family members to recognize criminal deceptive techniques, to ask questions, and to get involved in security. Just because a workman claims to be an electrician or is dressed in a telephone company uniform doesn't mean he is legitimate. Have outsiders provided your employees with any suspicious gifts such as wall clocks, calculators, pens, or potted plants? Do cleaning staff and unauthorized employees have unguarded access to sensitive areas? Keep in mind that dozens of listening devices have been planted by bribed or disgruntled insiders.

♦ Be sure that your building telephone closet (where all the telephone lines are located) is locked and inaccessible to unauthorized personnel. Security personnel should periodically check the closet for signs of forced entry. One listening device was discovered when an alert security guard noticed an alligator clip on one of the lines. Another device was discovered after a guard was unable to open a combination lock on the telephone closet. After cutting the original lock off, the eavesdroppers replaced it with a similar lock. A would-be eavesdropper was prevented from bugging a VIP's apartment telephone when the building engineer refused to accept a bribe and notified police.

♦ Support legislation that would require two-party consent on all taped conversations by private individuals. Most states currently only require one-party (usually the eavesdropper's) consent.

8

HOW PRIVATE IS OUR MAIL?

O f all the freedoms Americans enjoy, privacy of the mail is one of the most cherished. But how safe and how private is our mail? Are strangers reading our love letters, rifling through our business correspondence, or pilfering our personal mail? How much of our private mail is being stolen or stashed?

The good news is that most of our mail is safe, private, and delivered on time. The bad news is that over 200 million pieces of our mail is stolen, stashed, or snooped each year.

This means that unauthorized personnel are perusing 200 million letters containing financial, legal, and business information. Complete strangers are reading mail we send to friends and family. Millions of sympathy cards, thank-you notes, apology letters, wedding announcements, party invitations, and job proposals and inquiries are being opened by the wrong person.

During March 1997, I had an agonizing powwow with my accountant in order to figure out my 1996 taxes. Wrestling with mountains of financial data, we sorted through hotel, meal, and rental car receipts; invoices; canceled checks; medical expenses; telephone records; credit card receipts; and payroll vouchers. When the ordeal was over four hours later, I asked my accountant to send his completed product by certified mail.

"Where are my taxes?" I asked my accountant when my IRS forms had not arrived by April 10. "I mailed them two weeks ago," he replied. "I hand carried them to the post office . . . and I have the signed postal receipt right here in front of me."

Not wanting to be accused of filing late, I drove twenty miles to my accountant's office, picked up a new copy of my tax forms, and delivered them to the post office.

But the package my accountant mailed to me by certified mail, complete with a mountain of business and personal papers, has never arrived. Where is my IRS package? Is someone reading it? Will my very private and personal information be exploited? How does a certified package just disappear?

The sad truth is that I'll probably never know the answers to my questions. Even if I do find out, it will be too late; privacy once lost is irrecoverable. The only consolation is that I'm in good company.

In hundreds of known cases, mail has been stolen by employees of the U.S. Postal Service. And as the following three cases indicate, some of these dishonest employees steal thousands of letters and operate for years without getting caught or even arousing suspicion.

On May 7, 1994, members of the Long Grove Fire Department responded to a fire at a private residence in Palatine Township, Illinois. Since the owner of the home was at work, the firemen forced their way inside to extinguish the fire.

After dousing the flames in one upstairs bedroom, firemen opened the door to a second room to see if the fire had spread to other locations. That's when they discovered nearly one ton of stolen mail.

The owner of the home turned out to be Robert Beverly, a thirty-year-old U.S. Postal Service employee who had been delivering mail since 1987.

When postal inspectors raided Beverly's home, they discovered 3,423 pieces of first-class letters, 1,140 pieces of second-class mail, about 22,440 pieces of bulk business mail, and 4,364 compact discs intended for record club members. The discs alone were valued at $65,000. Beverly had been stealing the mail on his route for six years. "He's the best-read crook I ever encountered," quipped a Chicago police officer.

The loot found in Beverly's home was the eighth cache of undelivered mail discovered in the Chicago area during the first six months of 1994.

How could one letter carrier in one area steal a total of 31,367 pieces of mail without anyone getting suspicious?

A pack rat postman in Washington, D.C., was also discovered by accident. Trying to find the source of water leaking into a unit at the McLean Gardens condominium, maintenance workers entered an apartment owned by Robert William Boggs, a forty-six-year-old letter carrier. It was an assignment the maintenance workers will long remember.

Upon opening the door, the maintenance workers were assaulted by the foul stench of decomposing animals and animal excrement. Boggs had crammed his small efficiency apartment with forty-three live turtles, twenty-one dead turtles, sixteen live birds, nine dead birds, and a mixed-breed live dog who relieved himself whenever and wherever he pleased.

Boggs left water running on a plant in his kitchen sink, and it had overflowed, forming a small lake for both his live and dead pets.

Venturing forth with handkerchiefs over their faces, the workers soon discovered another prize; Boggs was hoarding thousands of pieces of mail in his apartment and a storage area.

Boggs returned to his apartment as postal inspectors were filling dozens of boxes with opened mail. Still wearing his blue postal uniform, Boggs was arrested, handcuffed, and escorted through a sizable crowd that had gathered in front of the building.

Inspectors needed four postal vans to haul the stolen mail away.

"I'm missing three letters and a bunch of photographs from my girlfriend," explained a twenty-eight-year-old man on Boggs's delivery route. "It makes me sick to think that weirdo had my personal letters and photos."

A dishonest mail carrier in Skokie, Illinois, would probably still be stealing and reading other people's mail if he had not been pulled over for a traffic violation.

As the police officer questioned Lowell M. Plost, who had been stopped for speeding, he noticed piles of mail—1,660 pieces of mail to be exact—in Plost's car.

The next day, postal inspectors raided Plost's home

and discovered an additional 6,455 letters hidden in his bedroom. We don't know how many letters Plost had stolen and discarded before the raid occurred.

Mail carriers Beverly, Boggs, and Plost are known to have stolen at least fifty-thousand separate pieces of our private mail. But none of these men were caught by design; all were caught by accident.

In the absence of a fire, an overflowing sink, and a speeding ticket, all three men would probably still be stealing our mail.

"I guess if you want your mail to be private, you'll have to send everything by registered mail," said Becky Boyd as she entered hundreds of mail theft incidents into my computer.

Instead of responding to Becky's comment, I simply handed her a pile of sixty-four incidents in which registered mail was stolen. Becky rolled her eyes, shook her head, and said, "What a world."

In the Midwest, authorities charged a postal employee with stealing bags of registered mail that contained silver bars, cash, plane tickets, personal letters, business correspondence, bank deposits, and food stamps. The complaint stated that in one and a half years, fifty-two bags of registered mail, containing $230,000 in valuables, had disappeared.

When postal inspectors and police searched the employee's home, they discovered eighteen bars of silver, $2,700 in cash, and empty envelopes matching much of the missing registered mail.

But not all undelivered mail is stolen; much of it is stashed and trashed.

Nationwide, there are hundreds of incidents in

which mail has been discarded by disgruntled postal employees.

"Why would a mail carrier throw the mail in the garbage?" I asked an experienced postal inspector.

"There are many reasons; but say you're mad at your supervisor, angry at the world, it's a hot day, and you want to go home to your girlfriend," said the inspector. "Well, you just throw all the mail in the trash, go home early, and feel good about sabotaging the system. But be sure you mention in your book that most mail carriers take great pride in protecting the mail and getting it to the customers," the inspector added. "Most mail really does get through, despite bad weather and biting dogs."

Searching for a Victoria's Secret catalogue on a Sunday afternoon, Susan Lamas, a twenty-six-year-old Good Samaritan, rummaged through a trash Dumpster in Washington, D.C. Instead of finding a catalogue, she found a bundle of sixty-two pieces of first-class mail that included a couple thousand dollars in rent payments and utility bills.

Ms. Lamas kindly delivered some of the checks and money orders to landlords and handed over the remaining mail to the postal officials.

Acting on a tip that mail was being tossed into a trash bin outside a post office in Washington, D.C., reporters with WUSA-TV decided to set up a concealed camera.

Later that night, television viewers watched as postal employees tossed bundles of supposedly undeliverable bulk mail into a garbage Dumpster.

Carriers are not permitted to destroy first-class letters that they cannot deliver, but they may destroy bulk mail, provided it cannot be delivered as addressed. But Dave Statter, a reporter respected for his professionalism, had no problem delivering a portion of the mail to the addressees. One mail carrier was fired and two were suspended.

On June 3, 1996, Wray Bragg noticed some unusual bags in a trash container behind the Hanover Commons shopping center in Virginia.

Opening the bags, Bragg discovered 1,550 pieces of mail containing corporate annual reports, invitations to social activities, government checks, and other important materials. Bragg immediately notified the U.S. Postal Service. A postal inspector handling the case, who had investigated six mail-dumping cases in other states, learned that the mail had been trashed by a temporary carrier.

While gathering material for this chapter, Victoria Brown, a researcher on my staff, asked an important question: "Who has access to our mail besides postal employees?"

Victoria's question led to another disheartening discovery; baggage handlers at airports frequently steal and rifle through bags of mail and invade our privacy by going through our checked luggage.

Although my company has recorded tens of thousands of crimes at airports, I was surprised at how much mail was stolen and how many bags were looted by dishonest baggage handlers. (See the list of incidents on pages 106–108.)

"We had a baggage handler who had some kind of an underwear fetish," explained the director of security at a large international airport in the Midwest. "He was going through women's luggage and stealing bras and panties."

I asked five women in my office if they would consider underwear theft as an invasion of privacy, and all five responded, "Absolutely!"

Dishonest baggage handlers invade personal privacy in many ways. "Thousands of passengers have had laptop computers, private videos, photographs, and briefcases stolen," explained the security director who asked to remain anonymous. "All those items, especially the computers, could contain materials deemed private."

Theft of mail by baggage handlers is by far the most serious and most common invasion-of-privacy offense at airports.

"Street robberies represent another threat to the nations' mail," said a postal inspector who has been assigned to offices in New York City, Chicago, and Miami.

The inspector wouldn't tell me how many mail robberies have occurred in recent years, but I document scores of cases each year.

On March 1 and March 4, 1996, in Tempe, Arizona, thieves broke into two U.S. Postal Service vehicles and stole thousands of pieces of mail. As with most postal vehicle robberies, the stolen mail included bills, personal letters, checks, bank deposits, food stamps, and business correspondence. Similar robberies of postal vehicles have occurred in every state.

Despite being the brunt of many jokes, the U.S. Postal Service is one of the most professional and efficient mail delivery organizations in the world. The vast majority of its employees are honest, extremely hardworking, and genuinely dedicated to keeping our mail safe. But until we prevent 200 million of our letters each year from being snooped, stolen, or stashed, we will not have privacy of the mail.

MAIL THEFT BY POSTAL EMPLOYEES

The following chronicle is a short sampling of cases in which postal employees have stolen mail. Although the author has recorded hundreds of incidents in which postal employees have committed theft, the exact number of dishonest employees is unknown.

1994—Washington, D.C.: Robert William Boggs, forty-six, a U.S. Postal Service employee, pleaded guilty December 22 to stealing thousands of pieces of mail. Boggs's secret was discovered when a maintenance worker entered his apartment to find the source of water leaking into the apartment below. Postal inspectors carted away dozens of boxes of undelivered mail, most of which had been opened.

1994—Illinois: On June 16, Robert Beverly, a Chicago letter carrier, pleaded guilty to stealing 3,400 first-class letters, 1,140 pieces of second-class mail, 22,440 pieces of bulk business mail, and 4,364 compact discs. The discs alone were valued at $65,000. The mail was discovered when fire-fighters responded to a fire at Beverly's home. It was the eighth cache of undelivered mail found in Chicago during the first six months of 1994.

1994—Virginia: Elvis Earl Askey, thirty-six, pleaded guilty in December to stealing 5,800 compact discs and sixty-six videotapes while working as a postal clerk at the mail distribution center in Merrifield.

1994—Pennsylvania: Eight people, including four employees of the U.S. Postal Service, were charged on March 15 with stealing thousands of pieces of mail. Postal inspectors discovered 2,000 pieces of undelivered mail in a letter carrier's van and home. The stolen mail included personal letters, business correspondence, compact discs, and videotapes. One of the employees stashed 234 first-class letters in the post office locker room, and another employee was caught hiding 335 pieces of mail in bushes.

1994—Texas: A twenty-nine-year-old postal worker in Harlingen was charged October 28 with stealing at least forty credit cards from the mail. Detectives believe that the woman stole the credit cards for her husband who is a crack cocaine addict.

1995—Michigan: Larry Leroy Hart, forty-three, a postal employee, was charged December 6 with stealing $230,000 worth of registered mail. The charges stated that since March 1994, fifty-two bags of registered mail were not delivered. The stolen mail included business correspondence, $68,000 in bank deposits, jewelry, food stamps, airline tickets, and cash. Inspectors found eighteen bars of silver, $2,700 in cash, and envelopes matching much of the missing mail in Hart's home.

1995—Maine: An employee of the state government was arrested and charged with stealing $500,000 worth of food stamps from the mail. Police believe that the suspect sold the stamps on the black market and may have been involved in thefts of other types of mail.

1995—Wisconsin: Police arrested a postal worker on March 27 and charged him with stealing sixty-seven U.S. Department of Military Affairs checks from the post office where he worked.

1995—Virginia: Tuyen Q. Le, thirty-three, a former letter carrier, pleaded guilty February 3 to stealing more than one thousand compact discs from a post office in Falls Church. Le would enter the post office during off hours and steal the compact discs that were sent by record companies to mail-order customers.

1996—Virginia: Gary E. West, thirty-two, a former CIA mailroom clerk, pleaded guilty to stealing more than one hundred agency credit cards and using them to run up $193,000 in expenses and cash advances. The credit cards were to have been used for CIA field operations.

1996—Illinois: Lowell M. Plost, a forty-six-year-old former U.S. Postal Service letter carrier, was convicted of stashing thousands of pieces of undelivered mail in his home and car. Chicago police discovered 1,660 pieces of mail in Plost's car in November 1994 when he was stopped for a traffic violation. The next day, postal inspectors found an additional 6,450 letters in Plost's bedroom.

1997—Minnesota: A former mail carrier was indicted for stealing credit cards from people on his route.

MAIL THEFT BY AIRPORT EMPLOYEES*

From 1987 to 1997, at least 388 airport employees were caught stealing from cargo shipments and passengers' luggage at airports in the United States. More than 100 of these individuals are known to have stolen U.S. mail. The following is a short sampling of mail theft cases.

1990—Metro Airport, Detroit: A Northwest Airlines employee was charged with stealing mail meant for nationwide delivery aboard commercial flights. The Northwest employee was the ringleader of a group of seven people who specialized

---

*Judging from the total losses, it is assumed that many more employees are stealing but not getting caught.

in stealing credit cards, blank checks, and credit card numbers found on bills or other correspondence.

1990—Hawaii: Twenty-two baggage and cargo handlers with Hawaiian Airlines were arrested and charged with stealing more than $500,000 worth of cargo, baggage, and mail from Hawaiian Airlines.

1991—Philadelphia International Airport: Two USAir employees were charged with stealing jewelry out of mailbags. The thefts occurred at Philadelphia International Airport and involved mailbags shipped by the QVC television shopping network. USAir is contracted by the U.S. Postal Service to deliver mail packages.

1993—Houston International Airport: Twelve current and former Continental Airlines employees were among fifteen people charged with stealing credit cards from mail shipments at Houston International Airport. All twelve employees were baggage handlers. The men were charged with stealing 176 credit cards, but thousands more have been stolen from the airport in recent years.

1995—Logan International Airport, Boston: A Northwest Airlines baggage handler pleaded guilty to charges of mail theft, possessing stolen mail, trafficking stolen credit cards, and conspiracy. The man was the third airline employee in five weeks to be caught stealing mail at Logan Airport. Although the group stole a variety of mail, they focused on envelopes they believed contained credit cards. The men stole at least seventy-five credit cards, which they used to purchase expensive trips and merchandise and obtain cash advances. Many of the intended owners of the credit cards suffered credit nightmares as a result of the thefts.

MAILBOX THEFTS

When it comes to security, perception has always played a powerful role. Put an expensive Rolex or Piaget watch on someone's wrist, and you see a beautiful, precision-made timepiece. A criminal looks at the same watch and sees a stack of one hundred dollar bills conspicuously dangling from some sucker's wrist.

When you look at a curbside mailbox, you probably see a functional but ho-hum container made of metal or wood. A criminal looks at that same mailbox and sees an unguarded, unlocked, safe-deposit box stuffed with diamonds and gold. He sees a hundred ways he can exploit you. He sees your soul.

On any given day in the United States, more than one hundred thousand residential mailboxes are burglarized by credit card and check thieves, stalkers, and a wide range of criminals interested in your personal, financial, legal, and medical correspondence.

Most of us would not dream of leaving $1,000 in cash in our mailboxes. Yet, as criminals well know, the items we place in our mailboxes every day are worth much, much more.

During December 1993, authorities set up a sting and were able to arrest forty individuals who had pilfered thousands of mailboxes in the Washington metropolitan area. Stealing credit cards and checks, the thieves absconded with about $10 million before being caught.

"Unfortunately, for every thief we catch, there are another fifty out there who continue to steal mail," said a postal inspector.

Although mailboxes are raided for many different reasons, thieves are especially fond of checks, credit cards, and preapproved credit card applications. Millions of checks and as many as 500,000 credit cards are in the mail every day.

When criminals steal preapproved credit card applications, they often fill them out using the victims' real names and addresses and then mail them back to the company offering the cards. A week or two later, the thieves raid the mailbox again, intercept the card, and embark on a spending spree.

Some people have had as much as $300,000 in credit bills charged under their names. Once fraud is proven, the credit card companies almost always cover the losses, but the victim may find himself in credit hell for months or even years.

Mailbox thieves operate in every community and in every state. In 1995, thieves had hit so many mailboxes in Arizona that Tony Kovaleski, a news reporter, aired a story on how consumers could help protect themselves from mail theft and credit card fraud. Then he went on a one-week vacation.

Shortly after returning, Kovaleski received a call from the Phoenix police saying they had stopped a man for a traffic violation and found a number of stolen credit cards in his possession. One of the credit cards belonged to Kovaleski. The criminal had stolen the card from Kovaleski's mailbox when he was on vacation.

"We didn't arrange for someone to take the mail out of the box while we were gone," Kovaleski told the *Arizona Republic*. "You cover stories like this and think, 'That won't happen to me.' And also, you think it won't happen in nice neighborhoods. I was wrong. It's happening everywhere, all over town."

Sometimes the police get lucky and discover mail they didn't know was stolen.

After a rash of burglaries in an upscale section of Bethesda, Maryland, police pulled over a driver who was moving slowly, signaling improperly, and did not seem to belong in the neighborhood. Police asked the driver and his passenger to get out of the car and were questioning them separately when the driver, a twenty-three-year-old security guard, blurted, "You can't stop us. We don't have any stolen TVs or VCRs in this car. You didn't see us steal that mail."

The astonished police officer then discovered piles of stolen mail in the man's car that belonged to a doctor and another resident who lived on a nearby street.

Arresting the two men, police would later charge them with stealing about $500,000 in TVs, VCRs, and other goods from homes in well-to-do sections of Maryland.

Police believe the two burglars took mail from overflowing mailboxes to get names, which they later called to be certain no one was home.

Many thieves will use a prop or a ruse to help them steal from mailboxes. In Hammond, Indiana, authorities arrested two men and a woman who stole mail from hundreds of homes in eight communities. Pretending to hand out promotional materials, the crooks went door to door distributing leaflets. While putting the materials in mailboxes, they would grab the mail inside.

Privacy of the mail is considered one of our most sacred rights. The following two sections are designed to increase awareness of this very serious problem and to help keep your mail safe from prying eyes.

A CHRONICLE OF MAILBOX THEFTS

1994—Maryland: Police arrested seven men, mostly from Nigeria, and charged them with burglarizing hundreds of mailboxes at apartment complexes and charging nearly $1 million on phony credit cards in the names of 500 innocent residents in Montgomery and Prince George's Counties. Using screwdrivers and butter knives to jimmy open mailboxes, the men allegedly stole financial statements, personal letters, and preapproved credit card applications.

1994—Michigan: Robert Wilber, thirty-five, pleaded guilty to cashing $133,000 in stolen checks made out to a University of Michigan professor and using the money for a six-week trip to Antarctica. Wilber stole the checks from the professor's mailbox, contracted a telephone answering service in the professor's name, used a mail drop service to establish a fake address, and set up a bank account in the professor's name.

1994—Texas: Thieves in Sugar Land, Fort Bend, and Missouri City stole checks from more than 120 residential mailboxes. Using a chemical solution that dissolves permanent ink, the crooks altered the checks' recipients, increased the amounts, but left the original signatures. The thefts of outgoing mail increased during federal holidays because people forgot that the mail would not be picked up.

1995—Washington, D.C.: The former boyfriend of a graduate student reportedly raided the woman's curbside mailbox for three months, stealing letters the woman sent and received from a new boyfriend. "He was clearly trying to sabotage my life," explained the victim. The man is suspected of flattening all four tires on the woman's car after reading in one of the letters that she was going to drive to the beach to meet her new boyfriend. Since the new boyfriend was receiving scores of harassing phone calls and had an unlisted phone number, it is assumed that the stalker also stole the woman's long distance phone bills. Two airline tickets, mailed by the boyfriend, mysteriously never arrived.

1995—Colorado: Postal inspectors arrested two men suspected of using several teenagers to cash tens of thousands of dollars in checks stolen from residential mailboxes. When arrested, the men had $48,182 worth of stolen checks in their possession. Operating between 11 P.M. and 4:30 A.M. the men would rifle mailboxes where the red flag had been raised to alert mail carriers to pick up outgoing mail. Stealing the checks residents used to pay bills, the men would erase the intended recipient's name, write in their own alias, and cash the checks.

1995—Maryland: After receiving tips from residents, a police surveillance team arrested two men who were part of a nationwide mail and credit card fraud ring. The surveillance team was set up after three residents complained of mail tampering. One victim gave police a description of a vehicle with Virginia license plates and provided the time of day the two men would drive to his mailbox and remove the mail. The men had applied for credit cards using the victims' names and addresses and were arrested when they returned to intercept the cards from the incoming mail.

1996—New York: A twenty-six-year-old man was charged with stealing federal income tax refund checks from several neighborhoods on Long Island. He was arrested after a bank teller became suspicious when he tried to deposit a $7,000 refund check. Investigators discovered that he had already forged signatures on $7,000 worth of checks.

1996—Michigan: Tracey Davis, twenty-five, was sentenced to ten months in federal prison for stealing mail from more than 200 rural mailboxes in western Michigan. She was ordered to repay $5,183 to her victims. Davis faces similar charges in Indiana.

1997—California: High school students walking home from school discovered and perused scores of opened letters, including extremely private personal letters and highly sensitive legal correspondence they found blowing in the wind. Police speculate that a mailbox thief discarded the letters when he or she couldn't find anything marketable inside. Many of the letters had been left in mailboxes for pickup. "I'm mortified," said a thirty-two-year-old woman who had half of a handwritten letter returned. "It was probably the most personal and private letter I've ever written to anybody. . . . I just know it's going to come back to haunt me."

1997—Florida: After transferring to Florida from Chicago, an airline hostess asked her psychiatrist to mail a complete copy of her file. The file never arrived. The woman, who had been raped by her own father, believes a mailbox thief stole her records.

Her mailbox was one of eleven in her apartment complex to be forced open and looted.

1997—Rhode Island: Police and federal authorities arrested four people who allegedly stole hundreds of credit cards and other mail from mailboxes and used them to purchase more than $1 million in goods. The mailbox theft ring operated for four years in East Greenwich, West Greenwich, Cranston, Barrington, and North Kingstown. The two ringleaders were forty-eight and fifty-eight years old.

PROTECTING YOUR PRIVACY

♦ After delivery, empty mail receptacles as soon as possible. Thieves frequently strike soon after the mail carrier has made his rounds.

♦ Gone are the days when you leave your mail in the mailbox and flip up the red flag. Outgoing bills and other important correspondence should not be left in your mailbox for the postal carrier. Such mail should be hand delivered to the carrier, dropped in a U.S. Postal Service mailbox, or carried to the post office.

♦ It is best if your incoming delivered mail is pushed through a door slot or placed in an area where it is inaccessible to outsiders. Mail

delivered to dormitories, offices, and apartment lobbies is often left unguarded and accessible to outsiders. Tell management that this
is irresponsible and unacceptable.

♦ Ensure that your mailbox is secured with a
strong lock. Locks that can be opened with a
screwdriver or a butter knife are unacceptable.
If you live in an apartment building, make sure
that the management changed the lock when
you moved in; you don't want the previous tenant to have access to your mail. It is preferable
to have a locked mail room; communal outside
mailboxes are particulary vulnerable.

♦ Report people loitering around mailboxes or
other suspicious activity. The postal service
sometimes offers rewards for information leading to the arrest of mail thieves. Remember
that thieves can be male or female, young or
old, well-dressed or poorly dressed. Try to get a
good description of suspicious personnel and
if possible the license tag of his/her vehicle. In
1996 alone, at least 210 mailbox thieves were
arrested because residents got involved and
helped police and postal inspectors.

♦ If you are going out of town, have a trusted
individual pick up your mail or ask the post office to hold off on delivery until you return.
Thieves love full mailboxes and an overflow signals burglars that you are out of town. Burglars

will frequently look at the names on the mail and then call that person to be certain no one is home.

♦ Don't be fooled by props or tricks. Using leaflets as props, many mailbox thieves go door to door pretending to hand out promotional materials. While putting leaflets in mailboxes, they grab the mail inside.

♦ Unprotected mailboxes outside large estates, where the boxes are far from the home or obscured by bushes and trees, are especially vulnerable. "Those are my favorite," said a thief arrested in Maryland.

♦ Keep a close watch on your bank and credit card statements. Make sure your checks match the statement and your checkbook and that they have not been altered. Be sure the charges on your credit card statement are accurate. If any of your monthly financial statements do not arrive, contact the appropriate bank or agency.

♦ Don't give out personal or financial information to a telephone caller. Purporting to be a banker or a detective, many mailbox thieves will call the victims they have burglarized and attempt to obtain the information needed to activate your stolen credit card or ATM card. They may claim a need to verify or update your records so they can better serve you. Since the impostors have stolen a great deal of information about you, they can sound very convincing.

9

PRIVACY AND THE IRS

On May 13, 1971, President Richard Nixon had a meeting in the Oval Office with aides H. R. Haldeman and John Ehrlichman to discuss the selection of a new commissioner for the Internal Revenue Service (IRS).

"I want to be sure he is a ruthless son of a bitch, that he will do what he's told, that every income tax return I want to see I see, that he will go after our enemies and not go after our friends," President Nixon told his aides.

The conversation is part of the 201 hours of secretly recorded Nixon tapes made public by the National Archives in early 1997.

Although the IRS has a moral and legal obligation to protect the privacy of taxpayers' records, thousands of people—including politicians, private investigators, and IRS insiders—have improperly perused private tax returns for personal reasons.

On July 18, 1994, Sen. John Glenn (D-Ohio), chairman of the Senate Governmental Affairs Committee, announced that more than 1,300 employees of the Internal Revenue Service had been investigated for using government computers to browse through tax records of friends, relatives, neighbors, celebrities, and complete strangers. It is not known how many IRS employees illegally perused tax records without being caught.

The 1,300 employees were either criminally prosecuted, forced to resign, or were reprimanded, suspended, or counseled, depending on the seriousness of their offenses.

Walter C. Higgins, a part-time worker at the tax processing center in Andover, Massachusetts, pleaded guilty to illegally obtaining tax information on Thomas Quinn, a Democratic candidate who challenged U.S. Rep. Martin Meehan in a congressional primary.

Geoffrey P. Coughlin, forty-six, culled through the confidential tax records of more than 150 people, including radio and television personalities, journalists, and former girlfriends, simply to satisfy his own curiosity. Coughlin was fined $3,000 and sentenced to two years' probation.

An IRS employee was convicted in 1995 of rifling through files of people he believed might be informants against white supremacist groups. The employee was also accused of reviewing the tax records of a black attorney who unsuccessfully prosecuted his father for the rape of a child.

"It scares and sickens me that a character like that would have access to my personal and financial records," said a forty-one-year-old female lawyer in Massachusetts.

In 1997, a federal appeals court overturned the former IRS employee's conviction, saying that the government had failed to prove that he had done anything with the information he gained by rifling through computer files.

The decision calls into question the convictions of Geoffrey Coughlin and other IRS employees in Massachusetts who pleaded guilty to looking at scores of tax records not assigned to them. Termed a browser by prosecutors, Coughlin is not known to have done anything with the information.

Many people are uncomfortable with the appeals court decision. "I don't care if a creep like that does anything with the information or not. . . . I'd still be uncomfortable with him looking at my private financial records," said the female lawyer in Massachusetts. "Besides, it's very easy for a rogue IRS employee to use the information in our files and very difficult to prove that he or she is using it for personal reasons."

"My neighbor is an IRS employee," said a woman in New Jersey. "Even if he doesn't do anything with the information, my income, investments, and tax records are none of his business."

The woman said that the IRS employee had asked her out for a date on four occasions, and each time she explained that she already had a boyfriend. "Is the court saying that it's okay for someone to stare at me in the shower as long as they don't do anything with the information?" asked the reporter. "I feel the same way about my tax records. If it's none of his business, I don't want my neighbor staring at my tax records."

W. J. "Billy" Tauzin, a Louisiana Republican and longtime critic of the agency, has described the IRS as "the most un-American agency we have in the country, where you walk in guilty and you stay guilty unless you prove you're innocent."

Historically, celebrities have been the most vulnerable to tax snoops. Hundreds of movie stars, politicians, athletes, CEOs, and other VIPs have had their private tax records disseminated to gossip journalists, nosy rivals, and other unauthorized personnel.

In 1996, Gov. William F. Weld of Massachusetts fired two welfare-fraud investigators for allegedly browsing the confidential tax records of three of Boston's best-known sports heros.

The pair left electronic fingerprints after calling up the tax records of Celtics great Larry Bird, Patriots quarterback Drew Bledsoe, and Bruins superstar Ray Bourque, all of whom are multimillionaires and far from being on welfare.

The Department of Revenue in Massachusetts was allowed access to computerized tax records as a tool for investigating welfare fraud, a problem that has cost Massachusetts taxpayers hundreds of millions of dollars. But as this case so aptly illustrates, it only takes one or two dishonest employees to put everyone's privacy at risk.

"The problem is that so many different employees have access to the information, and the data can be used in so many different ways," said a former IRS investigator. "We had cases in which confidential data was given to stalkers, mafia hoods, and even terrorists. . . . It's impossible to plug all the leaks."

Utilizing confidential information, many IRS employees have assisted criminals and endangered innocent lives.

In one case, a corrupt lawyer, employed by the U.S. Department of Justice, stole a 1,000-page Internal Revenue Service investigation and delivered it to the Detroit office of an alleged Mafia leader. In another case, police arrested a thirty-nine-year-old IRS employee and charged her with giving inside information to a gang of gun runners.

Approximately 56,000 of IRS's 115,000 employees have access to the agency's Integrated Data Retrieval System (IDRS). This system provides employees with taxpayer data such as name, address, Social Security number, taxable income, number of dependents claimed, and adjusted gross income.

But just because an employee doesn't have official access to the IDRS doesn't mean he can't obtain the information.

Lee Willis, an IRS clerk with a history of psychological problems, was obsessed with his twenty-three-year-old ex-girlfriend, whom he had been stalking for sixteen months.

Like many stalking victims, the girlfriend kept her address and phone number a secret, warned friends and neighbors to be on the lookout for her stalker, and tried very hard to make herself invisible.

Since Willis was not one of the 56,000 IRS employees who had access to taxpayer files, he persuaded a coworker to illegally search the computer and locate his ex-girlfriend's apartment.

Armed with his ex-girlfriend's address, Willis was able to gain access to a locked lobby by pressing apartment buzzers until an unwitting resident let him in.

Fearing for her life, the ex-girlfriend called police

and had Willis arrested. The police found a kidnap kit in Willis's car, consisting of a stungun, rope, latex gloves, duct tape, and a knife.

If a government employee is to be trusted with our most personal financial records, it is hoped that the individual would be honest and of strong morale and ethical character. But in dozens of known cases, IRS employees have proven to be as corrupt and unlawful as the worse tax cheats.

On February 9, 1997, in Cincinnati, IRS employee Reva G. Vanzijl, pleaded guilty to providing Social Security numbers to her brother and others, which allowed the gang to run up $8,700 in purchases on stolen credit cards. Vanzijl had been charged with providing privileged taxpayer information to unauthorized personnel, conspiracy, and aiding and abetting credit card fraud.

On April 19, 1997, the *Plain Dealer* reported that an IRS employee had been charged with lying to the IRS about her own taxes.

Prosecutors say that the employee provided auditors with phony letters, altered travel vouchers, and fictitious statements of charitable contributions to justify deductions on her 1990 tax return.

Although the employee could get a five-year prison sentence for making false statements to the government, a plea agreement allegedly reached with prosecutors guaranteed that she would be sentenced to no more than six months in prison and that she be eligible for probation if a judge agreed.

Perusing a long list of illegal acts by IRS employees—committed inside and outside the agency—I couldn't help but wonder if these same employees could be trusted with taxpayer confidentiality.

If an employee can rationalize theft, embezzlement, lying, and even violent crimes, that same employee would probably have no problem rationalizing invasion-of-privacy offenses.

Despite IRS promises to protect the privacy of citizens, voyeuristic employees continue to snoop at records.

On April 8, 1997, an IRS report to Congress stated that 23 employees had been fired, 349 had been disciplined, and another 472 had been counseled for unauthorized browsing through tax records during the last two fiscal years. The report also stated that the IRS could not account for 6,400 storage tapes and cartridges, some of which contained taxpayer data.

One week later, April 15, 1997, the Taxpayer Browsing Protection Act passed the Senate by a vote of 97–0 and flew through the house 412–0. Demanding zero tolerance, the act calls for a fine up to $1,000 and/or a year in prison for any IRS employee found snooping on citizens' tax returns.

In an effort to catch more tax cheats, the Internal Revenue Service is currently upgrading its computer system and vastly expanding the range of information it collects on virtually all Americans.

The new system is designed to help the IRS do a better job of enforcement, to collect an extra $100 billion per year from tax cheats, and to reduce tax burdens on low- and middle-income Americans.

But if the IRS expects to win the public's support and to do more good than harm, it will have to get a lot tougher on security, ensure the confidentiality of tax returns, and put a much greater emphasis on protecting taxpayer privacy. Unauthorized snooping is morally wrong, a precursor to corruption, and a threat to the very foundation of the voluntary tax reporting and collection system. Snooping should be an automatic firing offense, no excuses allowed, and should be further pursued in a court of law.

PROTECTING YOUR PRIVACY

- Income tax preparation firms and the IRS have a moral and legal obligation to protect the taxpayer's privacy. If you have information that a rogue employee is providing confidential information to unauthorized sources, notify the authorities. If you are not part of the solution, you are part of the problem.

- Get angry and get political. Urge your politicians to push for stiffer penalties for any employee caught snooping at tax records. Invasion of privacy should not be passively dismissed.

- Tax consultants and IRS supervisors need to be held accountable for the public's privacy. Employees should be given up-to-date briefings on computer security, regularly reminded to protect the confidentiality of tax returns, and in-

126

formed of the legal consequences if they do not.

♦ Many private tax firms have no way of knowing if an employee is snooping in computerized tax records. Databases containing confidential tax information should be set up so that no one can log on without leaving an electronic fingerprint that identifies the user. Supervisors need to keep track of who is using a file and why that file is being perused.

♦ If you know you are right, don't be afraid to fight the IRS. During the last five years, about 150 lawsuits have been filed against the IRS claiming wrongful disclosure of confidential information. On June 4, 1997, in Denver, Colorado, a federal judge awarded $250,000 in punitive damages to a woman whose family business was raided by armed Internal Revenue Service agents four weeks after the woman insulted an IRS agent. The agents asserted that the woman owed $324,000 in income taxes. After the raid, it was determined that the woman only owed $3,485, which she paid.

The agents padlocked all three Kids Avenue clothing stores in Colorado Springs and posted unjustified notices that some customers interpreted as evidence that the woman, Carole Ward, forty-nine, was a drug dealer.

Judge William Downes found that one agent was "grossly negligent" and acted with "reckless disregard" for the law and that he made three false statements to the court. The judge concluded that the IRS had violated Ms. Ward's privacy rights and had abused its authority.

After Ms. Ward paid the $3,485 in owed taxes and settled the case, an IRS district director went on a radio talk show and accused her, wrongly, of still owing $324,000 in taxes.

As for insulting an IRS agent, *don't be stupid!*

10

PRIVACY AND THE MEDICAL INDUSTRY

While conversing with a group of men and women in the lobby of an upscale health club, my attention turned suddenly to a new member, a strikingly beautiful woman, who had just walked by. "She's pretty, Lou, but you sure don't want to date her," whispered a woman who had been standing at my left shoulder. "She's got a screaming case of herpes."

Stunned by the cattiness and the inappropriateness of the woman's comment, I asked, "How do you know?"

"Because I work at the clinic where she's getting treatment," the woman nonchalantly explained.

Nowhere is invasion of privacy more common or more dangerous than in the health care business. In fact, with medical records becoming about as confidential as a listed telephone number, we are fast approaching a point where there will be no privacy at all.

Medical insurers, employers, crafty salesmen, direct-marketing companies, uninvolved employees of hospitals, and even nosy neighbors and coworkers now have the ability to learn the most intimate details about your mental and physical health. These people and others can find out your medical test results (have you ever had a sexually transmitted disease?), your medications (any drugs or medication for depression or hemorrhoids or birth control?), your family history for diseases (any Alzheimer's or mental retardation in the family?), and whether or not you have been raped or had an abortion.

A physician who gave birth at Beth Israel Hospital in Massachusetts was reportedly appalled to learn that ten curious but uninvolved colleagues had looked up her extensive medical history on the hospital computer system. In Philadelphia, a man who tested positive for AIDS discovered that his lab test results were listed in a hospital computer and that 100 employees not involved in his case had access to the information. The positive test result was leaked to the patient's friends and co-workers. A congresswoman in New York sued a hospital for $10 million after her attempted suicide was revealed during a political campaign. A hospital employee allegedly faxed her records to the *New York Post* and a television station.

Unfortunately, a hundred people can use a hundred different tactics to steal confidential medical information and then use that data in a hundred different ways.

In Florida, former patients of the Sarasota Memorial Hospital were furious to learn that hospital officials were providing their confidential medical, financial, and personal records to fund-raisers.

Florida law requires every patient's record to be kept confidential and states that private information can be released only with the patient's prior consent. But law and reality are two different things. Hospital administrators never notified the patients, never sought permission to release the records, and never obtained consent. Nor did administrators seek advice from their lawyers before releasing the private information to the Sarasota Memorial Hospital Foundation, Inc., an independent, direct-mail fund-raising organization. Instead, hospital officials saw a slick way to make a buck and charged ahead like the proverbial bull in a china shop. Approximately twelve thousand former patients are approached each year by the fund-raising group and asked to make donations.

The *Sarasota Herald-Tribune* uncovered the story and learned that Memorial Hospital was providing the foundation with instant computer access to the names, addresses, and medical conditions of the patients. In addition to the detailed medical, psychological, and financial information so casually released to complete strangers, the computer printout contained the patient's room number, prognosis, home address, admitting physician, discharge date, and data pertaining to family members.

The fund-raisers obtained the private information in two ways: First, hospital officials copied patient records, stored in a hospital computer, onto a disk. The disk was then loaded into the fund-raisers' computer and used for direct-mail solicitation. Second, the outside fund-raiser was allowed direct on-line computer access to the hospital's confidential patient files. The on-line hospital network was ostensibly set up for the sole purpose of helping physicians monitor and improve patient care.

A *Herald-Tribune* reporter quoted foundation president Ron Royal as saying that the on-line computer could provide him with "everything that's on the hospital admission list." Incredibly, Royal apparently felt justified in participating in this outrageous breach of public trust. "The only reason we have access to that information is so we can do our jobs better," he told the *Herald-Tribune*. "Our job is to raise money for the hospital."

But some former patients were spared the invasion of privacy; patients whose bill payments were overdue were not solicited for contributions. "Seems like the only way to insure confidentiality at Memorial is to be a deadbeat," joked a sixty-five-year-old former patient.

Despite well-intentioned pledges to protect privacy, unauthorized disclosure of medical records has become as common as colds. Informed consent has lost all meaning. Need to know now includes everyone, and doctor-patient confidentiality is fast becoming a thing of the past.

Two incidents that occurred in Florida and Massachusetts clearly illustrate how difficult it is to plug all leaks—and how dangerous it is when we don't.

In February of 1995, police in Florida arrested the thirteen-year-old daughter of a hospital clerk.

While visiting her mother at work, the girl got bored and used a hospital computer to print out a two-page list of patients who had visited the emergency room. The girl then telephoned seven patients from the list and informed them, falsely, that they had tested positive for AIDS.

One of the female patients, a married sixteen-year-old, became hysterical and tried to commit suicide after receiving the phony test results, but her husband and father were able to pry the gun from her hands. The patient's mother, who took the call, told the Associated Press that the girl said, "Her lab work is back, and I need to let you know that she's HIV positive. And she's also pregnant. You knew that, didn't you."

The sixteen-year-old had gone to the emergency room a few days earlier with a bladder infection and received a Pap smear and a pregnancy test. The lab later reported that she wasn't pregnant and had not been tested for the AIDS virus.

The girl was eventually sentenced to five years' probation and therapy for the prank, but the court proceedings still left many questions unanswered. Why was an irresponsible thirteen-year-old with a history of drug use, truancy, shoplifting, and other crimes given access to sensitive files? Why was it so easy for her to print out confidential information? Did her mother give her a secret computer password? If a thirteen-year-old girl has no problem stealing files, how secure is the hospital computer system?

An equally frightening incident that occurred at the Newton-Wellesley Hospital in Massachusetts demonstrates how one dishonest or disturbed individual can wreak havoc on thousands of lives. Mark L. Farley, thirty-four, who once raped an eight-year-old girl, was arrested on April 9, 1995, in Newton, Massachusetts, and charged under a new statute that makes it a criminal offense to use another person's password to gain access to a computer system.

The *Boston Globe* reported that Farley, who worked as an orthopedic technician making casts, allegedly used the protected password of a former hospital official to gain access to the confidential records of 954 patients, most of whom were young women and girls.

Farley allegedly perused these files and made obscene phone calls to a number of patients. His unauthorized access to the computer system went unnoticed for four months.

Since the hospital did not conduct a criminal background check on Farley as part of the hiring process, they were not aware that he had been incarcerated for assaulting and exposing himself to at least one little girl and raping another. Farley was released from parole in 1990 and began working at the hospital in 1993.

Is Farley the type of person we want working in a hospital? Should he be reading confidential files? Why didn't administrators deactivate the former hospital official's secret password? Farley allegedly perused 954 private files for four months without arousing suspicion. Why didn't the hospital conduct a routine computer search, or audit trail, to determine who and why the files were being accessed? Who else is reading our files? What else did Farley do with the files? Did he sell them to insurance companies, data bankers, or other sex offenders?

The exploitation of mental health files by psychiatrists, psychologists, and other mental health workers is another growing problem. Although no one knows exactly how many psychiatrists, psychologists, and counselors have exploited private information, my company has recorded 216 incidents in which mental health professionals have breached patient confidentiality.

Several mental health professionals have used confidential information for personal profit. On January 7, 1992, a court in New York fined Dr. Robert Willis $150,000 for securities fraud. While treating Joan Weill, Dr. Willis learned that her husband, Sanford, was trying to become head of BankAmerica Corp. by getting his former firm to invest $1 billion in BankAmerica. On the basis of that information, Dr. Willis bought stock in BankAmerica and made a $27,475 profit. In addition to the fine, Mrs. Weill filed a $5 million lawsuit against Dr. Willis for breach of confidence and contract.

In 1995, a Santa Monica psychotherapist pleaded guilty to insider trading for parlaying information gleaned during therapy sessions with a senior Lockheed Corp. executive into a stock market bonanza. The Lockheed executive was undergoing marriage counseling with Dr. Mervyn Cooper when he confided that Lockheed was negotiating a major financial deal. Just hours after the session, Dr. Cooper, fifty-seven, placed an order for 300 shares of Lockheed common stock.

Guilty of felony fraud, the psychotherapist agreed to pay $110,190 in penalties and returned profits.

Illustrating the dangers of erroneous mental health information, at least twenty-eight psychiatrists are known to have made up false diagnoses and fraudulently charged insurers for nonexistent therapy sessions. The phony diagnoses were entered into insurance databases and have come back to haunt many patients.

On August 2, 1995, a federal jury convicted Massachusetts psychiatrist Richard Skodnek for routinely making up diagnoses for patients he had never seen and fraudulently billing Medicare and private insurers $500,000.

One woman told the court that Dr. Skodnek falsely claimed to have treated her two children for severe depression. Quoted in the *Boston Globe*, the woman stated, "To think that somewhere in a big computer there's a psychiatric diagnosis of my kids. . . ."

Investigators admitted that it would be almost impossible to track down all the phony diagnoses by Dr. Skodnek that found their way into insurance databases.

In the era of computerized databases, it is impossible to devise a foolproof security system or to guarantee patient confidentiality. Even hospitals and insurers with the most stringent security controls are vulnerable to leaks and mistakes.

Legislation alone cannot stop the abuses. Technology alone cannot stop the abuses. Consequently, the public and the medical profession will have to remain forever vigilant if we expect to have any semblance of privacy.

MEDICAL DATABASES

Practically unnoticed by the public, the nation's health care industry is currently assembling an interlocking network of electronic databases—a master patient index—that will record every detail of your confidential medical history from birth to death.

Hospitals in the New York City metropolitan area have joined with three large health insurance companies to develop a medical data system that will trade information with hospitals, pharmacies, nursing homes, home care agencies, and doctors' offices. Another interlinked network being developed in Massachusetts will be accessible to tens of thousands of physicians, staff members, and others. Similar databases have cropped up in Chicago, Cleveland, Detroit, Los Angeles, Memphis, and a dozen other cities.

Supporters of the master patient index say that the system will bring better health care at a time when people are constantly changing jobs, changing doctors, and being shuffled from one HMO to another.

"The health care industry is now a giant conglomerate of hospitals, insurance companies, pharmaceutical firms, and associated networks of physicians," explained one health care expert. "If you want us to offer first-rate care and still run a sound business, then a centralized, computer-based master index is not only essential, it's inevitable."

The fifty-nine-year-old executive assured me that "we have the laws and the technology to keep records confidential," and rather condescendingly dismissed "privacy radicals" as a "bunch of paranoids resistant to progressive change." Considering that there have been four serious thefts of data at his own hospital, the executive's cavalier attitude concerning computer security is particularly disturbing.

Since tens of thousands of computer hackers, including frolicking teenagers, have been able to bust into the secure computer systems of law enforcement agencies, banks, government organizations, and groups like TRW, the credit reporting service, and Sprint, the communications company, what's to keep the same hackers from invading medical databases?

A Congressional study released in 1996 concluded that computer hackers attempted to break into Defense Department and Pentagon computer systems 250,000 times in 1995, and were successful in 65 percent of these "attacks." A separate study, conducted by the FBI and the Computer Security Institute, found that 40 percent of the 428 corporate, university, and government organizations surveyed reported at least one computer break-in within the last twelve months.

Using a common desktop computer, a teenager from the United Kingdom entered the Defense Department system and copied high-tech data from NASA's Jet Propulsion Laboratory and the Army's missile office.

"When we detect a hacker, we do an immediate damage assessment," said the condescending hospital executive who viewed privacy advocates as paranoid. So what! First, damage assessments are done *after* the damage is already done. How does that help the victims? Second, in most cases, you are not going to detect a hacker. The Congressional study concluded that even the security-conscious Defense Department detects only 1 in every 150 computer attacks.

What's to keep outsiders and dishonest insiders from stealing computers and disks containing confidential data?

At a large hospital in Florida two trusted security guards were arrested and charged with stealing three desktop computers. The computers contained the names of 7,000 patients infected with AIDS. The two security guards, who had the keys to several locked offices, were also linked to other thefts of computers at the hospital.

Thefts of computers is no small problem. Nationwide, approximately 208,000 portable laptop computers were stolen from offices, airports, cars, and homes in 1995. More than 100,000 desktop and larger computers were also stolen. Several thousand of these laptop and desktop computers, containing sensitive personal and professional data, were stolen from hospitals, clinics, and from medical doctors, nurses, and researchers.

When just one irresponsible researcher at one hospital loses just one computer, it can affect the privacy of thousands of individuals. As if to allay fears, many hospital administrators will explain, "Don't worry, only hospital employees have access to the information."

Once again we have to conclude, "So what!" There are literally thousands of known cases in which uninvolved medical employees perused private records for their own personal reasons and thousands of cases in which employees sold, manipulated, or exploited patient data for illegal purposes. And what about the cases in which private medical information was illegally exploited but was undetected?

A Colorado medical student was caught selling confidential patient records to malpractice lawyers. In Maryland, on June 13, 1995, authorities arrested twenty-four Medicaid clerks who tapped into the state's Medicaid computer databases and sold thousands of confidential patient records to private health maintenance organization recruiters. In South Carolina, a retiring doctor gathered 10,000 file folders containing his patients' records and sold them for $4,000 at a public auction.

Medical databases and individual records are valuable and marketable commodities. Computerized confidential records collected and stored by HMOs, public health departments, and hospitals are frequently purchased by private information companies. The personal medical records being sold include those related to mental health, drug and alcohol abuse, AIDS and other sexually transmitted diseases, and genetic histories.

Pharmaceutical companies snoop through medical databases in order to sniff out potential customers. The companies will market drugs for hypertension to people with high blood pressure. Insurance companies gather and purchase medical databases to determine who they should and should not sell policies to. One computerized clearinghouse provides medical and other risk information to about seven hundred U.S. and Canadian life insurance companies.

In one study, a researcher followed a patient's medical record from the time that patient entered the hospital until the time she was billed. The researcher discovered that eighty-six employees, including clerks and secretaries, had access to the patient's record.

Statistically, the vast majority of these employees will be honest, ethical, and professional. But security, like a chain, is only as strong as its weakest link. What is the probability that one to ten of the eighty-six employees would be dishonest and unprofessional? Unfortunately, the probability is very, very high.

The scariest consumer of medical information is the extortionist or blackmailer.

In Los Angeles, police arrested a Harvard University student and charged him with attempted extortion. The student allegedly demanded that a doctor who had tested positive for AIDS give him $10,000 or face public exposure. Sheriff's deputies grabbed the man outside a bar after he allegedly tried to pick up an envelope he thought contained the money.

"Some forms of blackmail are more subtle," explains a retired federal officer who worked on twenty-one extortion cases. "A politician would love to learn that his rival once visited a psychiatrist for depression."

In one case, a proabortion activist obtained the abortion records of a twenty-two-year-old woman who was the daughter of a religious leader staunchly opposed to abortion. Confronted with the illegally obtained records, the religious leader canceled a planned debate so that her daughter's medical records would remain private.

Our supposedly secure medical databases are as porous as sieves. Computers, with all their wonderful potential, are fast becoming the nemesis of privacy. It will be to everyone's advantage if we find a way to plug the security leaks and strike a balance between the care givers' need to know and the patients' right to privacy.

AIDS AND CONFIDENTIALITY

An employee of the Florida Department of Health and Rehabilitative Services (HRS) was fired in October of 1996 for what state officials called the nation's largest-ever security breach of AIDS information.

The employee, who had access to confidential computer files, was accused of removing disks containing the names of 4,000 AIDS patients and sharing the private information with unauthorized outsiders. An anonymous letter, sent to at least three newspapers, contained the 4,000 names and accused the employee of circulating the list in a bar and offering to look up names for friends who wanted to screen potential partners for HIV infection.

The case clearly illustrates the damage one unscrupulous employee can cause and throws a spotlight on new threats to medical privacy as computer hackers, insurance companies, and gossip mongers pry out the most intimate details of people's lives.

Confidentiality laws are designed to protect everyone's right to privacy and to shield the AIDS patient from harassment, discrimination, and blackmail. The laws also help to control and fight AIDS; if we do not assure confidentiality, fewer people will come forward for testing and fewer people with the virus will seek treatment.

Unfortunately, more than forty thousand HIV-positive individuals in the United States have had their medical records perused, stolen, and interpreted by unauthorized personnel. These illegally obtained records have been exploited by lawyers, political consultants, pharmaceutical companies, employers, insurance companies, and a wide range of gossip mongers, blackmailers, and homophobes.

A review of nearly eleven thousand cases indicated that there were three primary ways in which AIDS records were surreptitiously obtained: (1) trusted professionals blabbermouthed the information to unauthorized outsiders; (2) thieves, including trusted insiders, stole poorly secured files, computers, and computer disks containing AIDS records; (3) computer hackers gained unauthorized access to confidential databases.

Breaking the law, trusted professionals with loose lips have frequently leaked private information to unauthorized outsiders. These leaks have devastated the lives of hundreds of AIDS sufferers and their families.

On March 25, 1996, in Macomb County, Michigan, Stanley Grzadzinski, forty-one, sued the Troy-based Arbor Drugs and a prescription technician for allegedly gossiping about his HIV status.

Grzadzinski, who was diagnosed with HIV in 1990 but had no visible symptoms, alleged that the store prescription technician told her son of his condition and that the son told his classmates. The classmates then teased Grzadzinski's young son and daughter and reportedly called them AIDS babies.

Quoted in the *Detroit Free Press*, Grzadzinski stated, "I'm really concerned they're going to hurt my kids at school."

Mr. and Mrs. Grzadzinski had wanted to wait until his condition worsened before telling their children. Grzadzinski, who had a prescription for AIDS medication at the Arbor store said, "It should be up to the parents to tell the children, when they think the time is right."

In several known cases, insensitive teachers and professors released confidential AIDS information to students, fellow educators, and others. Some of these educators have been sued.

On May 1, 1996, in Montgomery County, Maryland, a teenage student (who is being called Courageous Youth to protect his privacy) filed a lawsuit against the Board of Education because a teacher revealed to his classmates that he was HIV-positive.

Students who are HIV-positive are not required to inform the school system, but the boy's parents notified the school's administrators in hopes that he would receive special help. The parents, however, made it clear that their child's medical information should be held in the strictest of confidence.

The boy's HIV status was allegedly revealed when a teacher saw some students sharing lip balm and warned them not to share it with Courageous Youth because he had AIDS. Courageous Youth, who was not in school that day, was said to have suffered extreme anguish, humiliation, embarrassment, shame, and emotional distress when he returned to classes.

Many trusted professionals (nurses, lab technicians, and pharmacists) who have a legitimate need to know have been conned into releasing confidential AIDS information to people pretending to be doctors, insurance company executives, and relatives of the patient.

"Susan is too scared and embarrassed to come in herself," said a private investigator who pretended to be Susan's father. "I was hoping to get her lab results so her mother and I could be the ones to break the news."

When misrepresentation doesn't work, many con artists will resort to bribery. "You'd be amazed at how many medical and insurance people will accept money for information," bragged the same investigator. "And always they say, you've got to promise not to tell where you got the information."

"The HIV virus stole my health," explained a thirty-one-year-old mother who contracted AIDS through a blood transfusion. "And when the hospital failed to protect my medical records, they stole my dignity and condemned me as a pariah."

UNSCRUPULOUS PHARMACISTS*

In order to perform a cost-containment analysis, the chief administrative officer of the South Eastern Pennsylvania Transit Authority asked a local Rite Aid pharmacy for a list of any prescriptions that exceeded $100 received by his employees. Wanting to please an important customer, Rite Aid sent the executive a long list of prescriptions ordered by his employees and even included their unsolicited Social Security numbers. Perusing the list of prescriptions, the executive noticed that someone had been receiving an anti-AIDS drug. The executive matched up the anti-AIDS drug to an employee's name and then shared the information with coworkers.

A jury initially awarded the employee $125,000 for emotional and psychological distress due to the breach of confidentiality, but an appeals court ruled that the

---

*See also "Aids and Confidentiality."

company had every right to the information, dismissing what it called "minimal intrusion" into the man's privacy.

How easy is it to find out if you have a prescription for an antianxiety drug, a birth control pill, or for a sexually transmitted disease? How easy is it to find out if someone is taking medication for AIDS, heart disease, or cancer? It's very easy. Using a wide range of legal and illegal tactics, thousands of unauthorized individuals obtain confidential prescription information from pharmacies and pharmacists each year.

Hoping to obtain titillating information on a well-known movie star, a reporter in California asked her pharmacist friend for a list of the actor's prescriptions. The pharmacist reportedly complied. In an upscale section of Washington, D.C., a pharmaceutical salesperson requested that a pharmacy provide him with a list of doctors who prescribe antidepressants such as Prozac, Zoloft, and Tagamet. The salesperson received a computer printout that included not only the names of doctors but the names of the patients for whom the drugs were prescribed. In New York, a self-described professional Dumpster diver retrieved a gold mine of prescription information by going through the trash at six pharmacies. Sifting through mountains of computer printouts, handwritten notes (apparently from orders that were called in by doctors), and other pharmaceutical records, the Dumpster diver claims to have compiled a list of over three hundred patients and their specific medications.

"I got the names of a big-time model, a television reporter, and twenty-two other people who have herpes," the Dumpster diver boasted. "And you wouldn't believe how many kids out there are taking Ritalin." Ritalin is frequently given to children diagnosed with attention deficit disorder. "I found five people taking antipsychotic medicine."

Although it is not clear what our Dumpster diver (a small-time hood and one of my former snitches) intended to do with his information, he does not strike me as someone who would be opposed to blackmail. "I even got the goods on a baseball player, a rabbi, and a big-shot banker."

Wanting firsthand evidence of the problem, I decided to test the security of a pharmacy in Maryland. After getting permission from a friend to use his name, I explained to the pharmacist that I needed a computer printout of all my prescriptions for the last year in order to get reimbursed from my insurance company.

The pharmacist could not have been more cooperative. Without asking for any identification, the woman smiled, said, "That's no problem," and printed out a long list of my friend's medications.

Alternating between anger, shock, and embarrassment, my friend commented, "Jesus! I definitely wouldn't want other people to know this information," and snatched the records from my hand.

As with all medical records, prescription information should be kept confidential. Licensed pharmacists and pharmacies need to understand how confidential information is being leaked, how the prescription data is being exploited, and correct the abuses. As citizens and consumers, we have the right to privacy.

GENETIC PRIVACY

Medical science has made huge advances in genetic testing. DNA probes can now gauge people's susceptibility to breast, colon, and prostate cancer and can unmask anomalous genes to determine if you or your offspring are likely to be stricken with maladies such as cystic fibrosis or Huntington's disease. Doctors, insurance companies, employers, and others are now able to predict which diseases are likely to show up in your future.

Genetic testing can do a lot of good. If identified early enough, some genetic maladies can be managed through medication and lifestyle changes. People who know that they have a high risk for cancer will be forewarned to the need for intensive monitoring. If a couple knows that they are carriers of a gene that will harm their children, they will be empowered to make better decisions about whether to have children. A Minnesota couple, for example, learned that they were the carriers of Tay-Sachs, a disease that causes death in children by the age of three. The couple decided to adopt a child.

But no one can guarantee the privacy of genetic information. Discrimination, therefore, is the inevitable downside to genetic testing.

Genetic testing has created a biological underclass consisting of tens of thousands of people whose genes have branded them as poor risks for health and life insurance, employment, and even marriage.

"She was definitely the girl of my dreams," a thirty-six-year-old doctor confessed to me. "But when a colleague told me that her father had Huntington's disease, I decided not to propose marriage." Huntington's is a disease that causes deterioration of the brain and dementia. A person afflicted with Huntington's has a fifty percent chance of passing the disease to his or her offspring.

There are thousands of cases in which genetic testing has led to some form of discrimination against the person who tested positive for a variety of diseases. In many cases, this discrimination affects an entire family.

In one case, a young couple took their six-year-old boy, who was having developmental problems, to a neurologist for a checkup. The neurologist determined that the boy suffered from a hereditary form of mental retardation and scribbled "Fragile X syndrome" on an insurance company claim form. Realizing that the incurable disease would cost them money, the insurance company immediately canceled coverage for the entire family of six.

Maria, a healthy, twenty-five-year-old graduate from an Ivy League college, told me that she was offered then denied a job in public relations after disclosing that she was deemed a high risk for breast cancer. "When they telephoned me with the bad news, the man said I was uninsurable," the woman explained. "But my rejection letter simply stated that other candidates were more qualified."

Most insurance companies will scour people's medical records, making sure there are no genetic land mines, before extending coverage. Almost any employer, school, research group, adoption agency, or data banker can get access—legally or illegally—to a worker's health data.

The explosion of genetic testing, in the DNA era, necessitates guarantees of genetic privacy and legal protection against genetic discrimination. Many privacy advocates believe that individuals ought to own all of their own genetic information and all the information that is derived from it.

Although thirteen states have passed laws designed to protect consumers' genetic information, we still have a long way to go if we expect to prevent discrimination.

STOLEN AND DISCARDED
MENTAL HEALTH RECORDS
— *Who Is Reading Your File?* —

After returning to campus following a long weekend, a university psychologist discovered that someone had rifled her office and cleaned out the top drawer of her filing cabinet. "I'm sure the cabinet was secured, but it had one of those cheap locks you can open with a butter knife," the psychologist admitted. The drawer contained the intimate, potentially embarrassing notes she had taken while counseling a student who had been sexually molested by her father, a student who had been gang-raped during an off-campus party, and a professor who was having difficulty dealing with his wife's affairs. "To this day, we are still agonizing over who could have stolen these files and how they might be used," the psychologist confessed. "One of my clients is the daughter of a celebrity, and police speculate that there might be a tie-in."

While walking to his home in Takoma Park, Maryland, John Schwartz, a reporter for the *Washington Post*, noticed that his neighborhood was littered with psychiatric records. Someone had tossed piles of these confidential documents into an overfilled Dumpster and a brisk breeze had distributed the papers in several directions. Collecting an armful of the papers, Schwartz noticed that they contained the names, addresses, and Social Security numbers of psychiatric patients. More importantly, the papers contained diagnoses, drugs prescribed, and extremely private, intimate details of these people's lives.

Poor office security and improper disposal of psychiatric records is a much greater problem than the general public realizes and is a violation of one of the most important rules of treatment: patient confidentiality.

Unbeknownst to trusting patients, thousands of sensitive psychological records are stolen or irresponsibly trashed each year, and a significant percentage of these documents are reviewed by people who have no business reading them.

Specializing in substance-abuse cases, Regent Hospital, a facility that serves upscale and high-profile patients, dumped boxes filled with patients' files on a busy New York sidewalk in 1994, where amused passersby picked through the contents.

The mistake reportedly occurred when a storeroom had to be cleaned out because of a major water leak.

A New York religious figure who had received help at the rehab center for alcoholism said, "I was furious. . . .

I had shared the most intimate and painful stories of my life with those people."

"I can't help but wonder who is reading my charts and whether the information will come back to haunt me," complained the clergyman. "And this breach of confidentiality could also affect my family. . . . I told the counselors private things about my parents and siblings."

With tens of millions of psychiatric records in existence and millions more generated every year, many medical facilities, in constant need of more space, become sloppy in the disposal of old records.

Workers at one mental health facility were told to replace several antiquated filing cabinets with a shipment of new floor-to-ceiling cabinets and to take the old ones to the dump. Unfortunately, the supervisor failed to tell the workers that before going to the dump, they should first take the files out of the old cabinets and put them in the new cabinets. The confidential psychological files were never recovered.

"Fearing lawsuits, management just stuck their heads in the sand and pretended the incident never happened," said a former employee of the facility. "To my knowledge, none of the patients were ever notified that their entire psychological histories might well be in someone else's hands."

Theft of files by a wide range of criminal opportunists is another serious threat to privacy.

Files that contained intimate and embarrassing psychological information concerning Princess Diana were stolen from her therapist's office in London. Princess Diana, a prime target of the gossip tabloids, was widely believed to have been grappling with deep depression during her rocky marriage to Prince Charles. The burglars may have obtained confidential records that documented Diana's alleged suicidal tendencies and her battle with the eating disorder, bulimia.

In Miami, Florida, during the weekend of March 2 and 3, 1996, someone crept into a six-story office building and ransacked State Senator Al Gutman's private, third-floor office. The burglars stole sensitive files, three computers, and diskettes containing information about a troubled HMO and extremely private medical and psychological data concerning the senator's constituents.

When it comes to theft of psychological records, ignorance, arrogance, and naïveté may very well be our worst enemies. Many mental health workers fail to comprehend that there truly are unscrupulous individuals and organizations who would benefit from their confidential case files.

Arrogantly dismissing advice that his office security was totally inadequate, a thirty-nine-year-old therapist in Washington, D.C., sneered defiantly and stated, "Oh please, I really don't think a burglar would be interested in these files."

Considering that the therapist's clients included two political types, a judge, and the CEO of a major organization, his cavalier attitude toward security was particularly disquieting.

Who would be interested in psychological files? Lots of people. And the list goes far beyond nosy neighbors, snoopy socialites, curious kooks, and inquisitive co-workers and in-laws.

When President Nixon's aides wanted to discredit Daniel Ellsberg, the man who leaked the Pentagon Papers to the press, burglars broke into a therapist's office and stole Ellsberg's psychiatric records.

During the last decade, stolen mental health records are known to have been used to embarrass politicians, to discredit witnesses and victims of crimes, to reject those seeking health insurance, and to blackmail at least a dozen citizens. Stolen files have been exploited by gossipy tabloid journalists, corporate executives, a wide range of unscrupulous lawyers and private investigators, and even by espionage agents.

"My psychiatrist's home office was burglarized," said a forty-three-year-old woman who was in the process of divorce, "then suddenly the details of my therapy were being used against me in my custody battle."

Confidentiality is to therapy what a sterile field is to surgery: a fundamental prerequisite to good practice. But there can be no confidentiality unless the therapist treats security seriously and disposes of private information in a responsible manner.

PROTECTING YOUR PRIVACY

♦ Think privacy! Without becoming paranoid, always ask yourself, "Who is going to see my medical information, and how might it hurt me?"

before filling out forms or offering information over the telephone or in person.

♦ Carefully read any health insurance or legal forms you are asked to sign that authorize the release of medical records. When you sign this type of form, you typically give up all confidentiality to the insurance company or law firm. Is there an unlimited time period for the release of information? Can the insurance company sell your information to data bankers? You can strike portions of the authorization, write a date of expiration, and add an addendum stipulating exactly who may see the information.

♦ Ask your doctor whether your medical records will be reviewed by people outside the practice. If the answer is yes, find out by whom and for what purpose. Does your doctor belong to a service such as the Physician Computer Network (PCN)? The network provides the doctor with a number of services in exchange for the right to copy patient information from the doctor's computer. If your doctor belongs to such a service, insist that he or she get your written permission before releasing your information.

♦ Be assertive about your privacy, and let others know you take privacy very seriously. Ask your doctor, employer, and insurance agent point-blank: "How do you protect my medical records?" Are your medical files and your personnel files kept together? If so, a person reviewing your personnel files could also peruse your medical files.

♦ Consider paying some medical and psychological counseling bills yourself to forgo reimbursement from your insurer. This will prevent your insurer (and the insurer's many contacts) from obtaining your private medical information.

♦ Responding to advertisements for medical products or free medical information might affect your privacy. People who answer these ads, which are found in publications and prescription drug packages, can expect to be targeted for direct marketing by pharmaceutical companies and other producers of health care products. One psychologist doing research on depression requested the free literature advertised in a prescription package. The psychologist later learned that the company had opened a marketing profile on her stating that she suffered from depression.

♦ Find out what the Medical Information Bureau (MIB) has on you. MIB, a nonprofit organization funded by 685 U.S. and Canadian life insurers, was formed to help companies detect fraudulent applications for health insurance. More than fifteen million people who have a serious medical condition or engage in high-risk behaviors, such as smoking, are on record with MIB. The MIB assumes no responsibility for the accuracy of its information, but it does allow you to request and correct your file. You may call the MIB at 617-426-3660 or write to: MIB, Box 105, Essex Station, Boston, MA 02112.

♦ Health employees should be instructed to be careful about what they place in the trash. Many of the most serious privacy infractions in the medical environment were the result of data that was improperly discarded. Administrators must develop and enforce a detailed policy for destroying and trashing sensitive information such as diskettes, computer print-outs, bills, and records. The policy should include instructions on what should be shredded, what should not be thrown in the trash, and who should handle and transport the trash.

♦ Hospitals, clinics, and private medical personnel would be well advised to have an experienced security professional conduct a security survey and evaluation of their premises. The officer should assess their physical and operational security and determine how effective that security would be against a wide range of criminal tactics.

♦ Filing cabinets containing confidential information should be housed in a secure office or room deemed secure by an expert. The cabinets should be of sturdy, top-grade material and should be secured with strong bar locks. Filing cabinets that can be opened with a butter knife or a screwdriver are not acceptable. To demonstrate poor security, I broke into one secure hospital storage area and opened two highly sensitive filing cabinets. The demonstration took three minutes.

♦ Private information should be discussed in private. A study reported in the *American Journal of Medicine* concluded that health care workers should be more careful about what they say in elevators and other public places. Researchers overheard inappropriate comments during about 14 percent of the 259 elevator rides they took in five Pennsylvania hospitals. The comments included derogatory remarks about patients and breaches of patient confidentiality.

♦ Be aware of the deceptive techniques that unauthorized outsiders might use to obtain information. In one case, a reporter pretended to be a patient's son in order to gather information for a story. The reporter secretly taped doctors, nurses, and clerks in private conversation. Several impostors have donned stethoscopes and white lab coats and pretended to be doctors. A wide range of unauthorized outsiders pretending to be police officers, relatives of patients, and insurance company representatives have conned hospital personnel out of confidential information.

♦ Verbal transactions between a receptionist and a patient should be as discreet as possible. Do not communicate Social Security numbers, insurance identification numbers, or private medical information out loud.

♦ If in doubt, don't give it out. Pharmacists, teachers, employers, nurses, and others should be very careful about divulging the sensitive medical information with which they have been entrusted. To tell a third party that someone has herpes or is taking an anti-AIDS drug is not only unconscionable, it could get you sued.

♦ Doctors and psychologists should not discuss sensitive patient information over a cellular telephone; outsiders often eavesdrop on this form of communication. Think before faxing private information. Is the intended recipient the only person who has access to the fax machine? Since many offices utilize communal fax machines, your communication might be read by unauthorized parties.

♦ Computer screens should not be visible to passersby. Depending on the sensitivity of your data, screens should not be facing an open window. There are cases in which undesirables peeked in ground-floor windows and used telescopes to observe screens and keyboards on higher floors. In one classified case, a hacker with a telescope was able to steal passwords by observing what letters were hit on the keyboards.

♦ Don't forget to log off when you leave your computer or are finished reviewing a file so that you don't leave the door open for unauthorized users.

♦ Hospital administrators should obtain software that allows only a few people the capability of changing or modifying data. There are dozens of cases in which unauthorized individuals have changed medical diagnoses, bills, and so forth. In an attempted murder, one disturbed individual entered a hospital database and changed a doctor's instructions concerning a critically ill patient. In 1994, a data supervisor at the New York City Health Department illegally changed the computerized results of an AIDS test from positive to negative.

♦ Administrators should conduct routine computer searches or audit trails to determine who and why files have been accessed. Look for red flags: the computer administrator should watch for high numbers of files being requested by one person, requests that seem inappropriate or unusual, and other suspicious activity such as requests for VIP files. One hospital employee was questioned about why he kept pulling the files of young children. Investigators learned that the employee was twice arrested for pedophilia.

♦ Theft of laptop and desktop computers poses a huge threat to medical databases and personal privacy. At least 208,000 laptop computers and more than 100,000 desktop computers were stolen in 1995. Employees should be briefed about this threat and educated about the importance of good personal security. A laptop locked in the trunk of a car, carried on a bus, train, or plane, or left in a hotel room is not secure. If the loss of a laptop computer would endanger or embarrass innocent people, it might be a good idea to keep it locked up. Computer users should protect their data with a password and use software that allows them to lock their keyboards and disable the hard drive before traveling. The same users should be advised, however, that experts can always find a way to enter those computer files through a back door, no matter how many precautions users take. The best advice is prevention; don't allow your laptop or desktop computer to be stolen, and don't download confidential information into portable computers.

♦ Instruct employees on the importance of protecting computer passwords. There are hundreds of known cases within the medical environment in which employees displayed secret passwords in public areas or shared passwords for access to confidential files with others. All too frequently, workers use easy-to-crack passwords such as their names. When an employee resigns or is fired, his or her password should be deactivated immediately. Passwords should be changed periodically.

♦ So-called talking computers that repeat spoken or typed information in a mechanical voice are not appropriate if privacy is a concern. One twenty-one-year-old woman whispered her name, Social Security number, and the very personal reason she needed to see a doctor to a clinic receptionist. When the receptionist entered the information, the computer repeated the very personal information loud enough for everyone to hear.

♦ Do not use Social Security numbers as the patient's insurance or medical identification number. Criminals have no problem obtaining Social Security numbers, and stolen numbers have already been associated with billions of dollars in theft and fraud.

♦ Support genetic testing laws that forbid genetic discrimination, protect genetic privacy, and ensure that the individual will give informed consent before undergoing DNA testing.

♦ Demand legislation that clearly establishes severe civil penalties and criminal sanctions for those who breach the privacy of medical records. These laws should also permit patients the right to review their records and to correct errors, just as they can with credit records. The laws should establish uniform federal rules for the use and disclosure of health information, specifying who may see confidential records and under what circumstances.

♦ Patients should be warned that there is always a privacy risk when medical records are computerized. Most hospitals are putting personnel data on line in such a way that many employees, including secretaries and people not treating the patient, can access the records. In a computerized system, information regularly crosses state lines and will therefore be subject to inconsistent legal and ethical standards with respect to privacy.

11

THE MISUSE OF LAW ENFORCEMENT INFORMATION

On July 8, 1996, the media disclosed that aides from the Clinton White House had improperly obtained the confidential FBI background investigations and personnel files on 400 Republicans. These files contained private information on U.S. citizens such as medical records, financial statements, and performance evaluations. As a former federal investigator, I am intimately aware that the files might also have contained unverified slanders, scurrilous rumors, and unconfirmed gossipy tidbits that investigators uncovered while interviewing the employee's neighbors, coworkers, friends, and lovers.

Shortly after the disclosure, FBI Director Louis Freeh said that his agency's unquestioning provision of the confidential FBI files to President Clinton's aides constituted "egregious violations of privacy" and he admitted that the White House had no justification for seeking the reports and the FBI had no excuse for providing them.

Partisan politics aside, the Filegate fiasco should be of concern to all Americans. Why was a totally unqualified and inexperienced individual like D. Craig Livingstone, a central figure in the scandal, entrusted with being the White House personnel security director? Why were political interns, volunteers, and other unauthorized personnel—many without security clearances—allowed to obtain and peruse the most sensitive and private of FBI documents? Why was the FBI unable to prevent the improper and illegal disclosure of private information? What happened to security standards?

As director of White House Personnel Security, D. Craig Livingstone was the official who allegedly ordered the 400 files from the FBI. What right would this thirty-seven-year-old man have in perusing your file or my file? How would someone like Livingstone interpret and use the contents of our files?

A political advance man, Livingstone has been described in the media as a bulky, blatantly partisan galoot who jumped from campaign to campaign performing minor roles for Democratic candidates. He reportedly attended a variety of colleges before graduating from the University of the State of New York.

Coworkers have been quoted as saying that Livingstone bullied anyone in his way, exaggerated his authority, and seemed unconcerned about the consequences of his behavior. An inexperienced person in a high-security position, Livingstone liked to give the impression that he was a Secret Service agent shouldered with cloak-and-dagger responsibilities. In reality, he was not authorized to carry a gun, did not have the authority to make arrests, and had no authority over the Secret Service. Ironically, the man who had access to the confidential FBI files on private citizens probably would not have passed the background investigation required to become a federal agent.

By his own account to the Government Reform and Oversight Committee, Livingstone had a history of using illegal drugs, had lied about his schooling (he claimed to have attended a college he never attended), and was mysteriously fired by a Sears Roebuck store for a questionable exchange of merchandise. Like many political appointees in security and law enforcement positions, Livingstone had virtually no relevant experience or qualifications for the job. He was apparently hired for the sensitive position because he listed on his résumé that he had supervised a campaign operation in which President Bush was heckled at a series of 1992 rallies by people dressed in chicken costumes.

Exploiting the power and perks of his office, Livingstone liked to drape gorgeous women on his arms and swagger around the White House with a self-important air.

In one case, reported by the *New York Times*, Livingstone sidled up to a pretty White House aide and began needling her about a prank from her college sorority days. He told her she would do fine as long as she did not "set off any fire extinguishers at the White House." Livingstone meant it as a joke, but the woman didn't laugh; she complained that he was abusing his access to her FBI file. Would Livingstone also make jokes and gossip about the information in our files?

Was the requisition of more than 400 FBI files on

honest, law-abiding, U.S. citizens part of a partisan smear campaign? Was D. Craig Livingstone compiling an enemies list? Perhaps we'll find out. On June 12, 1997, a federal judge allowed a lawsuit against the Clinton White House to go forward on behalf of Bush and Reagan administration employees who alleged the FBI improperly turned over their files for political purposes.

A high percentage of the 19,000 federal, state, and local law enforcement agencies in the United States have misused computerized criminal justice information and violated privacy regulations.

In Arizona, a former police officer gained access to the FBI's National Crime Information Center, tracked down his estranged girlfriend, and murdered her. In California, a Police Commission staffer used LAPD computers without authorization to get confidential data on political figures and celebrities, including Arnold Schwarzenegger. And in Pennsylvania, a police department employee used a computer to conduct background searches for her drug-dealer boyfriend, who wanted to learn if new clients were undercover drug agents.

The FBI's National Crime Information Center (NCIC), with 25 million records, is the nation's largest computerized criminal justice information system. Law enforcement agencies in the United States and Canada, using 98,000 computer terminals, have direct access to the system. Other systems that have been abused in the past include the Law Enforcement Automated Data System (LEADS) and the Interstate Identification Index known as the III file. All three systems include Social Security numbers, birth dates, arrest warrants, home addresses, and other information pertaining to private citizens.

Tens of thousands of private files from all fifty states have been illegally taken from police computers and sold to employers, insurers, lawyers, gossip mongers, political groups, and investigative firms.

From 1988 to 1997, at least seventy-nine sworn officers and civilian employees assigned to the Los Angeles Police Department were disciplined for misuse of department computers. Most of the offenders were selling the information to private investigators or simply snooping on friends, enemies, relatives, neighbors, or coworkers for private purposes.

Police records, illegally provided to outsiders, are frequently misinterpreted.

A hardworking Emergency Medical Service employee, who completed a Ph.D. by going to school at night, was mysteriously turned down for three different jobs. "They would tell me I had the job, then suddenly they'd hire someone else. . . . It was so time-consuming and frustrating," he complained.

When my company looked into the matter, we discovered that a civilian employee of a police department sold the man's record to a private investigative firm. The record stated that the man had been arrested for indecent exposure.

Although none of the would-be employers had bothered to obtain the details of the arrest, all three felt justified in rejecting the applicant. "We sure don't want someone who waves his penis at children," one administrator candidly admitted. "You didn't hear it from me," said another potential employer, "but he's a convicted sex pervert."

In truth, the indecent exposure arrest had nothing to do with sexual perversion. Seven years earlier, when the man was a college senior, he and several fraternity brothers were picnicking in a heavily wooded recreational park. After a couple beers, three of the men wandered back into the woods to urinate. As the men returned to the clearing, they were arrested for urinating in public. "You would have to have been a deer or a bear to have seen us," the man explained.

"Ten people could use pilfered police files in ten different ways," explained a former supervisor with the National Crime Information Center. "But believe me, for every person we caught misusing the system, dozens more got away with it."

A police dispatcher with a personal grudge used her office computer to harass a judge in Akron, Ohio. Gina Calvaruso looked up Judge Michael Callahan's home address using the Law Enforcement Automated Data System and then had *Playgirl* magazine mailed to his home and office. Quoted in the *Plain Dealer*, Judge Callahan said: "That was real embarrassing."

Calvaruso also filled out a change-of-address form that rerouted the judge's mail to the home of a defendant he had sentenced for child molestation. The dispatcher was angry with the judge because he had dismissed a civil case she filed against an insurance company.

Computer snooping and the misuse of criminal justice records occurs at all levels of law enforcement, from civilian clerks and secretaries to the chief of police.

During March 1997, prosecutors in Ohio charged a local police chief, with criminal misuse of the LEADS system.

The chief was accused of using the confidential statewide system to obtain information on politicians and opponents of the current mayor.

The computer snooping charges were dropped on March 5, 1997, when the chief agreed to resign from the police force within ninety days.

There have been many cases in which dishonest insiders have provided social and political activists with confidential information, a violation of state and federal laws.

On June 29, 1993, the Los Angeles Police Department announced they were investigating allegations that one or more officers had rifled confidential records and provided them to the Anti-Defamation League. The report outraged Arab-Americans and other U.S. citizens who felt that their privacy rights had been violated by the collaboration of a law enforcement agency with the ADL.

Soon after the announcement, the *Los Angeles Times* reported that Roy Bullock, an investigator for the ADL, admitted receiving driver's license and criminal history information on about fifty people. Police then raided Bullock's home and found additional confidential data in his computer. Bullock reportedly admitted that he sold some of the police information to the South African government.

From 1987 to 1997, at least 4,400 civilian and sworn law enforcement personnel are known to have used confidential criminal justice information for unofficial purposes. Most of this information was passed along to private investigators, political activists, lawyers, and other unauthorized personnel who, in turn, provided the data to third and fourth parties.

Since many dishonest employees have stolen hundreds of private files—and most offenders are never caught—it is reasonable to assume that millions of Americans have had their criminal justice files perused by unauthorized personnel.

A CHRONICLE OF ABUSE

1992—Maryland: An investigator for the county Child Support Enforcement Division was indicted on charges that he accessed confidential computer databases to run a business selling information to private clients. The employee was charged with using state computers for eighteen months to obtain the whereabouts, criminal histories, and employment income of private citizens for his clients.

1993—New York: Neal Elefant, an Orthodox Jew, translated wiretaps of conversations in Hebrew into English for the FBI. After two months on the job, he learned that another Jew was the target of a $15 million money-laundering scam. Feeling he had a moral obligation to warn the suspected criminal, Elefant stole FBI documents, set up a meeting with the alleged criminal, and alerted him to the investigation. Prosecutors would later tell the judge that Elefant had jeopardized agents' lives by warning the alleged criminal. The judge handed Elefant an eighteen-month prison term.

1994—California: Former LAPD Deputy Chief Daniel R. Sullivan, once considered a top contender for the chief's job, pleaded no contest to illegally possessing confidential law enforcement information. He received a $4,995 fine and was sentenced to a year's probation.

1994—Texas: Robert Davis, a former Hidalgo County sheriff's deputy, pleaded guilty August 2 to selling federal criminal history information to a private investigation firm. Davis was paid $27,000 by an Atlanta-based company to supply information he gleaned from the National Crime Information Center, which is run by the FBI.

1994—New Jersey: A former investigator with the Essex County prosecutor's office was dismissed from his job and sentenced to three years' probation for selling confidential FBI criminal records to the owner of a private security firm in Washington State. He was also convicted of conspiring to access a federal computer without authorization. The investigator was the fourteenth person to be convicted in 1994 in the government's investigation of what prosecutors called infobrokers.

1994—Maryland: An FBI clerk was indicted on two counts of bribery for allegedly providing confidential information to unauthorized personnel in exchange for $400. The woman was fired for revealing information from the FBI's computerized database.

1994—New York: Two detectives, in separate precincts, were arrested and charged with selling confidential law-enforcement information to organized-crime figures. Both detectives were assigned to the department's Organized Crime Control Bureau that handles the most sensitive undercover investigations. One of the detectives had been investigating Colombian drug traffickers but had access to confidential Mafia information through computers. Investigators assigned to the two cases noted that there had also been other recent instances of state and Federal insiders selling secrets to criminals.

1995—Pennsylvania: On April 27, the chief of a police department was charged with stealing highly confidential information from the FBI's National Crime Information Center and selling it to private investigators. The alleged thefts occurred over a four-year period and included printouts from the Interstate Identification Index. The stolen data included state and federal criminal records, aliases, fingerprint classifications, and a great deal of personal information that was designed to be used and interpreted by authorized law-enforcement agencies only.

1995—California: On August 8, prosecutors charged a retired Los Angeles police detective, two private investigators, and a fourth person with allegedly using an LAPD computer to obtain confidential records, which they sold to private clients. The confidential material included driver's license photographs, customer billing records from telephone companies, personal credit reports from credit agencies, and customer account records from a local bank.

1997—California: Two Los Angeles police officers were charged with illegally accessing criminal records from the LAPD confidential computer databank for personal use.

12

PRIVACY SHORT STORIES

Strip mined by infobrokers, databankers, and gossip-mongers, privacy in the United States is silently eroding and is fast becoming an endangered national resource. As the following short stories will indicate, privacy is not one issue; it is a hundred issues.

HOW PRISONERS STEAL OUR PRIVACY

In California, a woman was obsessively stalked by a man who threatened to kill her and rape her young daughter. When the man was finally sent to prison for murder of an apartment manager and rape of an eleven-year-old girl, the woman moved to an undisclosed location and was relieved to finally be safe from her stalker. But the incarcerated stalker wrote a letter to the Department of Motor Vehicles claiming that the woman was a witness to an accident. Incredibly, the DMV sent the woman's undisclosed new address to the prisoner. The DMV clerk even put the prisoner's ID number on the envelope.

Making matters worse, the prisoner filled out a change of address form in the woman's name, mailed it to the postal service, and was able to divert the woman's mail and tax returns to his prison cell.

Without exaggeration, there have been tens of thousands of cases in which prisoners have been allowed to invade the privacy of innocent, law-abiding citizens.

In one case, a prison work-release program had inmates keypunching confidential medical records into a computer system. The prisoners were given access to the private medical records of thousands of unsuspecting women and men. One of the inmates, a convicted rapist, used the information to stalk and harass a twenty-five-year-old woman. The woman had been seeing a psychiatrist because she had endured years of rape and sexual abuse by her father. In another case, a convicted pedophile in a Minnesota prison compiled a computerized database of more than five thousand children and babies, all annotated with descriptions like "Little Miss pageant winner," "cute," and "latchkey kid." The database had been pieced together from information gleaned from small-town newspapers and was stored with child pornography the prisoner obtained over the Internet.

More than 4,000 people in the United States have had their identity stolen and their good credit ruined by prisoners who obtained their credit card numbers. The inmates used the credit card numbers and prison telephones to order millions of dollars worth of merchandise.

In the space of fifteen months, inmates at Graterford Prison in Pennsylvania ordered more than $2 million in televisions, computers, jewelry, and clothes using stolen credit card numbers. Accomplices on the outside obtained the numbers from hotel trash bins and then gave the numbers to the inmates.

Identical scams have been reported at a dozen other maximum-security prisons in the United States.

"I am so sick of the system that cares more for the rights of criminals than for victims," said a thirty-three-year-old Maryland man who was victimized by an incarcerated murderer.

Private and public companies are increasingly turning to prisoners for data entry projects. Inmates in twenty-eight states are currently given access to public records like motor vehicle registrations and Internal Revenue Service data and are being allowed to input this information into computer systems. Prisoners are also handling and inputting information that millions of honest citizens volunteered in surveys.

HOW SURVEYS STEAL PRIVACY

Surveys are not always what they claim to be. A front-page article in the *New York Times*, June 12, 1997, told the story of how Beverly Dennis from Massillon, Ohio, was victimized by a survey she filled out. It showed how information ostensibly collected for one reason can be reused in entirely unanticipated and even detrimental ways without the knowledge or consent of the individuals who provided the data.

Ms. Dennis, who is in her fifties, came home from

work one evening and found a letter with a Texas postmark from a complete stranger who seemed to know a great deal about her. The stranger knew her birthday, her favorite magazines, and the soap she used in the shower, and he communicated this information in a twelve-page, handwritten letter that included threatening sexual fantasies.

The letter-writer was a convicted rapist and burglar serving time in a Texas prison. How did the prisoner know so much about Ms. Dennis? She had filled out a seventy-seven-question consumer survey on the promise of coupons and free samples. How did a rapist gain access to the survey? The product questionnaires that Ms. Dennis and millions of other unsuspecting citizens filled out were delivered by the truckload to the Texas prison system, which reporter Nina Bernstein discovered was under contract to handle the surveys for the Metromail Corporation, a leading seller of direct-marketing information. Hundreds of unpaid inmates had been recruited to enter the information into computer systems.

When Ms. Dennis hired a lawyer to sue Metromail, she learned that Metromail had a twenty-five-page dossier on her. The company knew her income, that she was divorced (a rapist or burglar might assume she lives alone), her hobbies, and her ailments. They knew if she wore dentures and how often she used room deodorizers and remedies for hemorrhoids and yeast infections.

Metromail claims that they did nothing wrong and that Ms. Dennis has no reasonable claim to privacy because she volunteered the information in consumer surveys.

IS SOMEONE PEEKING AT YOU?

The eight female lifeguards at a YMCA in Pennsylvania just knew something was strange; their male supervisor always told them when to take a shower and then disappeared. The womens' instincts were right on target. The supervisor had installed a two-way mirror above the bathroom sink in the women's locker room, which afforded a view of the showers and toilets. Detectives observed the man disappear behind a crawl space and caught him sitting in a chair and looking through the mirror.

Two-way mirrors and peepholes have become a serious threat to privacy. From January 1987 to January 1997, at least 347 illegal peepholes and two-way mirrors were discovered, usually by horrified victims, in public rest rooms, store dressing rooms, locker rooms, and other locations. In many cases, hundreds of women, men, and children were victimized by a single peephole or two-way mirror before it was discovered.

Scores of peepholes and two-way mirrors have been discovered in hotel rooms.

A mother and daughter discovered peepholes in their hotel room in Tennessee. Their attorney stated, "The only reason for the peephole being there is for employees of the hotel to watch people undressing, showering, or involved in sexual intercourse." In South

Carolina, five hotel guests discovered employees staring at them through peepholes. A jury awarded the victims $10 million, which a judge reduced to $500,000. And a newlywed couple, interviewed on a popular talk show, explained the horror and revulsion they felt when they discovered that they had been watched through a two-way mirror in the honeymoon suite at a major hotel.

Many of these public peepholes and two-way mirrors have been used by rapists, kidnappers, and murderers.

At 3 P.M. on a fall day in 1995, a woman we'll call Debbie Reston set out with her nineteen-month-old daughter for a children's clothing store in her neighborhood. At 9 P.M., Reston's husband reported his wife and daughter missing.

Police later arrested the son of the store owner, and charged him with the murders of the mother and daughter. A classic sex offender who reveled in pornography, peeked at disrobing children, and fondled unsuspecting women, the suspect told police where they could find the strangled and beaten bodies.

Police found blood and hair allegedly belonging to the victims in the clothing store and in the suspects's car. He had deep scratches on his face and arms.

In searching the store, police also discovered peepholes in the children's dressing rooms.

PEEPING TOM STALKER

In 1993, a twenty-five-year-old woman moved from Arizona to Colorado to enroll in the anthropology department at the University of Denver and to escape Steve Gordon, thirty-five, who had been obsessively harassing and stalking her. Shortly after moving into the Sunburst apartment building in Denver, the woman discovered, to her horror, that Gordon had moved into the same building. Several days later, the victim spotted Gordon in the anthropology department office at the University of Denver, and her fear mounted.

The woman would later tell the court that she had hoped to find privacy and safety at the University of Denver but that Gordon had violated her sanctuary. "I couldn't get away from him, wherever I went."

On January 28, 1994, the woman left the Sunburst apartments in a state of terror after finding a hole drilled through her bathroom floor.

A maintenance man at the Sunburst apartments, who caught Gordon in the crawl space beneath the apartment building, found the hole that had been drilled through the bathroom floor. He also noticed that the floor beneath the bathroom vanity was loose and could be removed. This enabled a person to view the bathroom and living room area.

Gordon remained free after the bathroom incident, but the woman obtained a restraining order directing him to stay away from her new home and places of work. During the next few months, Gordon repeatedly violated the restraining orders.

On March 20, 1995, Gordon was found guilty of ten stalking and Peeping Tom charges.

Stalking and peeping are two of the most insidious affronts to privacy.

WHO'S LOOKING OVER YOUR SHOULDER

In 1994, police in Illinois arrested a man accused of peeping on fifteen women and girls and entering the unlocked bedroom window of an eleven-year-old girl. The suspect reportedly picked his victims randomly at stores and libraries and got their addresses by peering over their shoulders while they wrote checks or checked out books.

Thousands of privacy offenses and other crimes each year are the direct result of an offender peering over an innocent citizen's shoulder or overhearing a pertinent conversation.

Two-abreast seats on subways, buses, and airplanes were not designed with privacy in mind. It is not only impossible not to hear what your seatmate is saying, it's difficult not to see what he or she is writing or reading.

It is, therefore, not advisable to write private letters, pay bills, balance a checkbook, or study confidential client information in a public area.

If you read magazines that have been mailed to your home, it's a good idea to remove the address label; criminals have utilized the addresses on magazines to target scores of unsuspecting victims.

CATCHING A PEEPING TOM

A woman in Stuart, Florida, called police thirty times over a five-year period to complain that a man was peering in her window and masturbating. Each time she complained, the police explained that they didn't have the manpower to do surveillance. Afraid for her life, the woman was forced to sleep in a locked room with a powerful handgun within easy reach.

Angry that police would not help her, the woman concealed a video camera inside a shirt and set it in a laundry room outside her condominium. The camera caught a young man peeking into her kitchen window and masturbating.

The police were able to identify the exhibitionist as a result of the videotape. He was arrested and eventually pleaded no contest to a misdemeanor charge of exposing his sex organs.

Peeping Toms invade the privacy of millions of Americans each year.

MISTRESS TAPED HOUSING SECRETARY

The *New York Times* reported on September 22, 1994, that Linda Medlar, the former mistress of Henry G. Cisneros, the Federal Housing secretary, had secretly taped telephone conversations she had with the secretary during their three-year extramarital affair. Medlar reportedly sold the tapes to the television show *Inside Edition* for a sum reaching five figures.

When the tapes were released, Cisneros was forced to admit that he paid Medlar more than $50,000 in 1993, in apparent contradiction of his public statement that payments had ended by the time he joined the Clinton cabinet. Transcripts from the tapes quote Cisneros as describing President Clinton's leadership style as indecisive and referring to FBI agents as "gossipers and scandalizers" who are "real bad at tracking down financial things."

Mr. Cisneros, a rising star in the Democratic Party, first acknowledged his relationship with Ms. Medlar in 1988, when he was still mayor of San Antonio. Ms. Medlar was a former campaign worker.

Ms. Medlar, who was unemployed when the secret tapes were released, was suing Secretary Cisneros for $256,000 for further support. She claimed he broke an agreement to pay her $4,000 a month until 1999.

At one point on the tape, Ms. Medlar warns Secretary Cisneros, "Honey, I'm as smart as they come. I know exactly what would do you in."

After reconciling with his wife, Cisneros still made payments to Ms. Medlar totaling $200,000.

SEVEN-YEAR-OLD TAPES TEACHER

Drew Carrier, a seven-year-old living in Sapulpa, Oklahoma, told his mother that his second-grade teacher was mean, but the mother wasn't sure whether to believe her son or not. So the mother told her second-grader to hide his Fisher-Price toy tape player in his backpack and secretly record his teacher.

"I can't wait till next year when some of you get to third grade. I can't wait," the teacher could be heard yelling to the class. "About half of you will be making F's."

As the young boy played more of the ninety-minute tape, the mother could hear the teacher scolding a pupil for bothering a classmate: "That's probably why you can't read very well."

After hearing the tape, Delynn Carrier and another mother moved their children to another classroom and requested that the teacher be fired. Mrs. Carrier reportedly said she wished her son had taped every lesson and complained that the teacher was hurting the students' self-esteem.

FIRE CHIEF TAPE-RECORDED FIREMAN

Claiming their privacy was violated, eleven firefighters in the Midwest filed a $5 million lawsuit against the fire chief, their boss, because he allegedly tape-recorded personal phone conversations on firehouse phones. The chief was placed on a five-day unpaid leave after city officials confirmed the taping.

Under the applicable state law, eavesdropping on a private conversation without consent of those who use the lines is a felony.

The taping was discovered in February 1996, when a firefighter found a cassette on the seat of the chief's car and played it.

Firefighters, who complained their privacy had been invaded, were furious that the chief would listen to conversations with their spouses and loved ones. Firefighters suspect phone calls were tape-recorded during protracted union negotiations with the city.

POLICE WATCH STRIP SEARCH

Three male police officers in Massachusetts received five-day suspensions without pay, in 1997, because they allegedly watched a teenage girl being strip-searched at the police station on a television monitor.

The men reportedly switched the television monitor from multiscreen view to one screen so they could watch a female officer conduct the strip search. An independent witness and the female officer reported that the violation occurred.

The police department's internal affairs unit concluded that the officers had no right to witness the search, and that by their actions, they violated the girl's right to privacy.

CAMERA CATCHES CORRECTIONAL OFFICIAL

"None of us is above the law," said Judge Peter Leavitt as he sentenced Martin Sekulski, a former captain in the Department of Corrections in Westchester, New York, to probation and community service.

Captain Sekulski, forty-three, admitted on October 1, 1994, that he induced two male inmates to engage in sex acts with him.

Unbeknownst to Captain Sekulski, the sex acts were filmed by a prison security camera and were watched by wide-eyed correctional officers who saw the incidents on a television monitor.

TAPING CONFESSION TO PRIEST

On January 29, 1997, a federal appeals court ruled that the surreptitious tape-recording of an inmate's sacramental confession to a Catholic priest in an Oregon jail violated the religious freedom and civil rights of both men.

The April 1996 confession, held in the Lane County Jail in Eugene, Oregon, was taped without the knowledge of the priest, Rev. Timothy Mockaitis, or the prisoner, Conan Wayne Hale. Catholics are taught to believe that confessions are completely confidential.

Hale was a suspect in a triple homicide of three teenagers who were found naked and shot through the head at the end of a remote logging road.

Oregon state law, and that of many other states, allows jail conversations to be taped without the consent of anyone involved. The only exception made is for conversations between an attorney and client. But another Oregon state law, which is in apparent contradiction, guarantees the confidentiality of conversations between clergy and the congregant.

After a local newspaper revealed the taping incident, it caused a public uproar, especially in law enforcement and religious circles, that even reached the Vatican. The Vatican sent a formal note of protest to the U.S. government.

The contents of the confession, which were made public, revealed that Hale professed his innocence to the priest. Hale, who may have guessed that the confession was being taped, told the priest that his friend and codefendant, Wayne Susbauer, had actually committed the murders.

MICROPHONES AT FAST-FOOD SHOPS

You might want to think twice before you engage in a personal or sensitive conversation at a Dunkin' Donuts; the walls may have ears. In 1994, the media reported that hundreds of Dunkin' Donuts shops and thousands of other restaurants in the United States had installed hidden microphones capable of picking up customer conversations.

After reports that monitoring was widespread in the doughnut shops, the company decided to ask the franchises to end the practice. But that doesn't mean monitoring will automatically stop; independent owners can ignore the request.

The harsh reality is that thousands of fast-food outlets, restaurants, and retail stores have concealed tiny electronic ears in secluded places. While these devices do have a benefit for security, there is nothing to prevent a gossip monger from utilizing overheard conversations for personal reasons.

HIDDEN CAMERAS AT PEPSI-COLA

Many Pepsi-Cola employees at a plant in Twinsburg, Ohio, were outraged when a hidden camera the size of a car cigarette lighter was discovered in the men's bathroom and locker area.

A company spokesman said the surveillance was for unspecified security reasons. Furious workers called it an invasion of privacy.

A union steward removed the camera and asked a shift supervisor about it. The supervisor was reportedly speechless and refused to comment on the camera.

On May 23, 1997, the American Management Association released a study that concluded that two-thirds of employers record employee voice mail, E-mail, or phone calls, review computer files, or videotape workers. The study, which surveyed 900 companies, also found that 25 percent of the companies that engage in surveillance don't tell their employees.

SECRET VIDEOTAPING BY PHOTOGRAPHERS

A photographer in New Hampshire was arrested in February of 1997, and charged with luring teenage girls to his studio with tempting offers of money and modeling careers. The middle-aged photographer allegedly persuaded the girls to pose nude and videotaped himself having sex with a fifteen-year-old girl.

When police raided the photographer's studio, they found videos, photographs, and other evidence that indicated that women and girls had been secretly videotaped while changing clothes. Clients who did not know a camera was hidden in the dressing room were instructed to remove undergarments to avoid unsightly bulges and lines.

The author has recorded more than eighty instances in which models and would-be models were secretly videotaped while changing clothes in a dressing room.

BANKER EXPLOITS MEDICAL RECORDS

People who claim that medical records are safe are often naive about how such records can be obtained and exploited by unauthorized personnel. In Maryland, a wealthy banker gained access to a list of cancer patients because he was a member of the state health commission. The banker compared that list with loan records at his bank and called the loans of patients with cancer. Is this the type of person we want on the state health commission? Is this the type of person we want as a banker?

A University of Illinois study found that half of Fortune 500 firms acknowledged using medical records in employment decisions.

"We offer good money to anyone who can provide us with potential employee medical records," a senior vice president of a communications firm boasted.

PATIENT FILES ON USED COMPUTER

When C. J. Prime, a self-employed computer technician in Pahrump, Nevada, purchased a used IBM computer for $159 at an Internet auction, she got more than she bargained for. When she turned on the computer, she discovered 2,000 patient records from Smitty's Supermarkets pharmacy in Tempe, Arizona.

All the software that the pharmacy had used for record keeping was still on the computer's hard disk, including patient names, Social Security numbers, addresses, and a list of all their medicines. The records showed prescriptions for AZT for AIDS patients, Antabuse for alcoholics, as well as numerous antidepressants and psychotropic drugs.

Ms. Prime once lost a job after an employer discovered she suffered from multiple sclerosis and is now an advocate for patient privacy.

Using the purchased computer, a skilled operator would probably have been able to connect to the pharmacy's main office and change records, order or change prescriptions, and cause other problems.

ABOUT THE AUTHOR

LOUIS R. MIZELL, JR., is an expert on criminal and terrorist tactics, targets, and trends and has been featured on dozens of television shows including *Oprah, Good Morning America,* and the *Today Show.*

As a former special agent and intelligence officer with the U.S. Department of State, Mizell served in eighty-seven countries including such hot spots as Lebanon, Iran, Chile, Colombia, Peru, and the Philippines. In addition to his investigative and intelligence roles, he was assigned to Secretary Cyrus Vance's personal protection team, protected Senator Nancy Kassebaum in El Salvador, and worked at both the 1984 and 1988 Olympics.

Mizell also served in Vietnam with the United States Marine Corps, has a master's degree in law enforcement from American University, and is author of several books on security and crime including *Street Sense for Parents, Street Sense for Students, Street Sense for Seniors,* and *Street Sense for Women.*

He has received over a thousand invitations to speak on topics of terrorism and crime throughout the world and has taught a graduate course on terrorism at American University. Mr. Mizell is currently president of Mizell and Company, International Security, a group in Bethesda, Maryland, that collects criminal and terrorist data on four thousand topics.

Heterick Memorial Library
Ohio Northern University

DUE	RETURNED	DUE	RETURNED
OCT 21 1998	5 1998	13.	
2.		14.	
3.		15.	
4.		16.	
5.		17.	
6.		18.	
7.		19.	
8.		20.	
9.		21.	
10.		22.	
11.		23.	
12.		24.	

WITHDRAWN FROM
OHIO NORTHERN
UNIVERSITY LIBRARY